EXCELLENCE IN BANKING

By the same author

THE EURO-BANK: Its Origins, Management and Outlook
THE MANAGEMENT OF INTERNATIONAL BANKS

EXCELLENCE IN BANKING

Steven I. Davis

St. Martin's Press   New York

© Steven I. Davis 1985

All rights reserved. For information, write:
St. Martin's Press, Inc., 175 Fifth Avenue, New York, NY 10010
Printed in Great Britain
Published in the United Kingdom by The Macmillan Press Ltd.
First published in the United States of America in 1985

ISBN 0–312–27359–2

Library of Congress Cataloging-in-Publication Data
Davis, Steven I.
Excellence in banking.
Includes index.
1. Bank management. I. Title.
HG1615. D39 1985   332.1′068   85-18341
ISBN 0–312–27359–2

To the excellent managers who made this book possible

Contents

Preface ix

1 THE EXCELLENT BANKS: SELECTION AND PROFILE 1

2 VALUES AND CULTURES 14

3 STRATEGIC DIRECTION 33

4 PRODUCTS: DIVERSIFICATION AND INNOVATION 41

5 CUSTOMERS: SEGMENTATION AND PROXIMITY 53

6 ORGANISATIONAL STRUCTURE 65

7 LEADERSHIP: THE CHIEF EXECUTIVE'S ROLE 74

8 HUMAN RESOURCES: THE CARE AND FEEDING OF EXCELLENCE 83
   8.1 Selection 84
   8.2 Training 88
   8.3 Career planning and performance review 93
   8.4 The reward system 96
   8.5 Human resource issues 100

9 RISK CONTROL 103
   9.1 Credit risk 103
   9.2 Interest and exchange rate risk 114
   9.3 Funding risk 115

10	**SUMMARY: THE CHARACTERISTICS OF EXCELLENCE**	117
	10.1 An open culture	118
	10.2 Strong shared values	119
	10.3 Profit performance as a value	120
	10.4 A customer-driven orientation	121
	10.5 Willingness to invest in new products	121
	10.6 Strong and consistent leadership	122
	10.7 Commitment to recruit the best people	123
	10.8 Investment in training and career development	124
	10.9 A matrix-based management information system	124
	10.10 A strong and balanced credit process	125
11	**OUTLOOK: THE NEW GLOBAL CHALLENGES**	128
	11.1 Break-up of the family	129
	11.2 Pay for performance	130
	11.3 More recruitment of outsiders	130
	11.4 Higher educational standards	131
	11.5 Greater emphasis on non-credit products	132
	11.6 Focus on funding	133
	11.7 More effective cross-selling	133
	11.8 Focus on technology	134
	11.9 Entrepreneurship and bias for action?	135
	11.10 A testing of the culture	136

Index of Bankers 139
Index of Subjects 141

Preface

There are no prizes for guessing the event which stimulated the writing of this book. Reading *In Search of Excellence*, by Robert Waterman and Thomas Peters, was a signal event in my 25-year involvement in commercial banking as a bank analyst, middle manager, chief executive and now management consultant.

Throughout this career unresolved questions have circulated through my mind. Are bank managers different from managers of other businesses? Is banking as badly managed as many observers feel it is? How well are banks dealing with environmental change? And can outsiders manage banks better than the insiders who have traditionally sat in the top-corner office?

And here are Messrs Waterman and Peters deliberately excluding banks from their sample of excellent institutions! Here is a pathfinding, challenging volume widely acknowledged – by bankers and millions of other readers – as a thoughtful framework for management action, but which once again seems to confirm that banks are beyond the managerial pale.

This smoking tinder was ignited by the Egon Zehnder survey in 1983 which confirmed that there indeed did exist excellent banks – at least in the US and in the judgement of their American peers. From then on it was a question of seeking confirmation and reassurance from a number of old friends: Bill Turner of McKinsey in London; Tim Farmiloe, my most supportive and positive editor at Macmillan; Robin Monro-Davies of IBCA Banking Analysis; Charley Williams of the Harvard Business School: John Rudy of Greenwich Research Associates and others who eventually made up my selection panel.

Then came the agony of waiting for the responses to letters to the chief executives of the sixteen chosen banks. Would they give of their time and support the project? With very few qualifications, the answer from the likes of Dr Wilfried Guth, John Medlin, Curt Olsson and Lew Preston was a strong affirmative.

And so the book was launched. My first two efforts as a writer on bank management, as I acknowledged in the preface to the first, did not progress far from the reinventing-of-the-wheel stage. They described how banks – good, bad and indifferent – run their business. This one goes a bit further. Here are acknowledged banking leaders describing how they are different from their peers. The last two chapters of the book, where the author tries to synthesise and pull threads together, may well be regarded as yet more motherhood and apple pie. But it is the apple pie of a dozen or so top management teams speaking openly about how they run their businesses. Can the outside observer do better?

My thanks therefore go to the fifteen panel members who were able to make transnational choices of what constituted global excellence, and to the managements of the sixteen banks themselves for having created a tradition of banking excellence – and taken the time to tell the world about it. And finally, a vote of grateful thanks to Dolores Mulroy, who once again translated my scrawl into something comprehensible to an IBM PC.

London STEVEN I. DAVIS

1 The Excellent Banks: Selection and Profile

The purpose of this book, quite simply, is to determine whether any patterns of excellent management practices can be identified by empirical analysis in the commercial banking sector.

That splendid volume by Robert Waterman and Thomas Peters, *In Search of Excellence*, has provided such a framework for non-bank corporations. Are banks different? If so, how? Are there any conclusions from using a comparable analytical approach which would help bank managements to do their job better?

There are some very good reasons why no one has yet tried to crack this particular nut. First, the managerial track record of banks as a whole is hardly outstanding. A fairly widespread view of senior bank management goes as follows: a sector only recently emerging throughout the world from regulated public utility status; an in-grown culture where successful lenders are promoted to senior management jobs for which they are ill-equipped; a focus on traditional deposit and lending products when a tidal wave of financial services evolution is about to descend; and, worst of all, belying their vaunted credit skills by making a mess of LDC lending. As another banking consultant puts it, how can you ignore all those bum loans to Latin America when they are at least supposed to know how to lend money?

A second obstacle is the definition of 'excellence'. How can we possibly define such a piece of jargon? What kind of statistical test could be used to define a credible sample when one tries to compare banks coming from totally different markets as well as varied natural or regulatory advantages. Is it really fair to compare a Rust Bowl with a Sun Bowl bank, a retail with a wholesale, and so forth? Another problem is the time dimension. Halls of Banking Fame looked at in retrospect justifiably cause a bit of jollity as they invariably include several names who have subsequently become badly unstuck. Five years ago this effort in an American context would undoubtedly have trawled up a Continental Illinois, SeaFirst, Interfirst or other subsequently fallen angel.

One last obstacle was erected voluntarily. *In Search of Excellence* chose to deal only with US firms: analysing non-US companies poses obvious problems of comparability. Having observed banks in a variety of national markets as a banker and consultant over a career of twenty-five years, however, the author decided to step in where angels had feared to tread. The internationalisation of banking and the apparent spread of management practices – not just lending to Latin America! – across borders seem to justify taking a global look at banks.

This means having to deal not only with the cultural/structural/economic discontinuities which deterred the McKinsey authors but also the obvious problem of statistical comparison. One might conceivably compare a Rust Bowl and Sun Bowl bank, but juxtaposing a Japanese or Swiss institution as well should be recognised even by a junior bank analyst as a statistical folly.

Somehow these obvious pitfalls only moved the project along to the next step. Not even advice from colleagues that any selection process was bound to annoy banking friends and clients was a sufficient deterrent.

The next step was to select an analytical process. One possibility would be to apply the *In Search of Excellence* framework directly to banks. This has merit, but it would be a straitjacket if, indeed, banks turned out not to be like ordinary corporations. Another would be a more rigorous and scientific process by which two samples – one excellent, the other deplorable – were selected and compared to determine the basic differences. This has the merit of logic, but the extra interview work and volumes of readily available material on the latter category argued in favour of a third approach.

This technique essentially involves analysis of a selected sample of presumably excellent institutions to identify the characteristics which underpin that quality. It is essentially the open-ended, subjective approach of the McKinsey authors with commercial banks throughout the world as its universe.

The time had now come to attack the problem of selection, bearing in mind the pitfalls outlined above. The issue of data comparability on a transnational basis quickly eliminated any hope of using a statistical screen for this purpose. Profound differences in disclosure, tax and accounting practices and the total illogic of comparing banks from different peer groups torpedoed the idea of selecting a top cut in terms of traditional bank evaluation criteria such as Return on Assets and Return on Investment.

There remained the use of a panel of independent professional observers with a transnational knowledge of commercial banks around the world. Bankers were excluded from the panel so as to obtain a totally unbiased view from individuals whose professional focus is the evaluation of bank management. Those individuals whose knowledge is truly global are few, but an extended search resulted in a selection panel of fifteen which includes leading financial journalists, management consultants, regulators, senior rating agency officers, experienced bank credit and securities analysts based in the US, UK and Western Europe. The charge to them was an open-ended one: to select ten commercial banks which they considered to be among the best managed in the world. It was left to them to define management excellence. Several found it hard to identify ten such institutions. Others raised the same caveats discussed above but eventually produced the desired list.

There were obvious definitional problems. Small regional or community banks were excluded for a variety of reasons – one of which was that they might not have had to deal with severe competition. Only institutions whose principal business is the taking of deposits and lending of money were included, so that British merchant banks like Warburgs had to be excluded. All votes were tallied, and those banks receiving more than a significant minority of panel votes were selected.

The list of excellent banks thus include the following:

Bank of Tokyo Ltd
Bankers Trust New York Corporation
Barclays Bank PLC
Bayerische Vereinsbank AG

Citicorp (Citibank NA)
Deutsche Bank AG
HongkongBank
Morgan Guaranty Trust Company of New York
Security Pacific Corporation
Skandinaviska Enskilda Banken (S-E-Banken)
Sumitomo Bank Ltd
Swiss Bank Corporation
Texas Commerce Bancshares, Inc
Toronto Dominion Bank
Union Bank of Switzerland
Wachovia Bank and Trust Company, NA

One other bank received the minimum number of votes but declined to be interviewed.

With the list in hand, the project now seemed to make sense. Honest observers can disagree honestly about the inclusion or exclusion of individual banks, but those receiving the most votes *do* roughly reflect the conventional wisdom of the banking world and its various constituencies. With few exceptions, all panel members picked Morgan, Deutsche Bank and Citicorp. Others selected by more than half of the panelists were Security Pacific, Swiss Bank Corporation, and Sumitomo Bank. Interestingly enough, a 1983 survey by Egon Zehnder International of over 3000 US bank chief executives picked Citibank, Morgan and Wachovia as the three best managed US banks.* Deutsche Bank is universally acknowledged to be the leader among the major German banks – if not *all* major European banks. Murmurs of dissent understandably grow as one moves down the ranking. Had a Zehnder-type worldwide poll of bankers been taken, however, the final profile would probably not have been radically different from this one produced by a limited number of highly qualified professionals from outside the banking community.

Having said this, one must acknowledge the limitations of any such arbitrary and imperfect selection process. There is absolutely nothing sacred about this list. Our goal is simply to select a group of banks which is *perceived today* (at the end of 1984) by some informed observers to be particularly well

---

* National Banking Survey of Chief Executive Officers, carried out by Egon Zehnder International in Atlanta, Georgia, November 1983.

managed. The law of averages – and the sad experience of past embarrassing 'Banker of the Year' awards – almost ensures that one or more of these banks will have egg on its face at some time in the future. What is important is to detect possible common patterns of excellent management practices among a decent sized sample of institutions.

Experience in banking – as in most other businesses – is that one can do just about everything right but that one horrible mistake can jeopardise one's image if not solvency. Perhaps none of these sixteen banks does *everything* right, but a mosaic of good management practice should emerge from verbal dialogue and a thoughtful analysis of behaviour. Even a partial and imperfect set of sound practices could add value to a bank management struggling with deregulation, competition and other terrors of the 1980s.

What is the statistical profile of this sample? Table 1.1 provides a summary of descriptive, as opposed to normative, information. From this data emerges a rough profile of the banks' size, product range and customer base.

There is a wide distribution by national origins. Six of the banks are American – an acknowledgement of the physical importance of the US banking market as well, perhaps, as the leadership role played by some US institutions in the practice of bank management. There are two banks each from Japan, Germany and Switzerland, which seems to reflect the size of these markets as well as the central role played by banks in their national economies. Hong Kong, Canada, the UK and Sweden are each represented by a single institution. Conspicuous by their absence are banks from several major European countries as well as the non-OECD world.

Most of the banks are large, if not mammoth, in size. Of the top 100 commercial banks in the world in asset size as measured by *The Banker* (June 1984), a total of fifteen figure in Table 1.1. Three of the world's ten largest are excellent institutions. The only representatives of the 'regional', or middle sized category, are Texas Commerce and Wachovia. While one might regret the relative absence of smaller institutions, analysing how managements of larger banks have dealt with the problems posed by physical size must be a useful exercise. One of the critical issues addressed by *In Search of Excellence* is the management of size, which is particularly

TABLE 1.1 Description of excellent banks

Bank/Group	Total assets end – 1983 (in $billion)[1]	Number of branches or other operating units[2]		Product range	Number of employees[1]	Assets per employee ($ million)
		Domestic	Foreign			
Bank of Tokyo	65.0	34	34	Commercial (d)* Universal (a)*	14 700	4.42
Bankers Trust Co.	37.0	4	23	Commercial (d)* Universal (a)*	11 700	3.16
Barclays Bank	94.1	2900	2300	Universal	123 000	0.77
Bayerische Vereinsbank	41.6	400	10	Universal	13 000	3.20
Citicorp	126.0	← 2600[3] →		Commercial (d)* Universal (a)*	63 700	1.98
Deutsche Bank	76.8	1349	23	Universal	47 300	1.62
HongkongBank	58.0	432	633	Universal	44 100	1.32

Morgan Guaranty Trust	56.2	8	29	Commercial (d)* Universal (a)*	13 000	4.32
S-E-Banken	20.4	356	5	Universal	7 400	2.76
Security Pacific	38.6	1200	100	Commercial	26 800	1.44
Sumitomo Bank	101.1	216	14	Commercial (d)* Universal (a)*	13 800	7.33
Swiss Bank Corporation	48.2	197	25	Universal	14 300	3.37
Texas Commerce	19.0	65	2	Commercial	7 900	2.41
Toronto Dominion	32.7	983	15	Commercial	17 600	1.86
Union Bank of Switzerland	52.8	241	17	Universal	17 200	3.07
Wachovia Bank	7.5	202	1	Commercial	6 500	1.15

(d)*Domestic.
(a)*Abroad.
[1] SOURCE *The Banker*, June 1984.
[2] SOURCE IBCA Banking Analysis and Annual Reports.
[3] Includes representative offices.

relevant for banks as they compete with smaller, more entrepreneurial and flexible institutions such as merchant and investment banks.

In terms of products, there is a good spread in the excellent sample from purely commercial banks at one extreme, through the US and Japanese institutions struggling with domestic legal constraints, to the classic universal banks of Continental Europe offering a full panoply of securities-related and other investment banking products. Chapter 4 will examine this dimension in some detail.

Customer profile is shown in Table 1.1 by the bank's ratio of assets per employee and branch office configuration. Pure wholesale (or corporate) banks are represented by Morgan, Bankers Trust and Bank of Tokyo, while all of the others have a major retail (or personal banking) as well as wholesale capability. Assets per employee range from the retail-oriented Barclays' $770 000 to Sumitomo's remarkable $7.33 million. Chapter 5 deals with issues of customer selection, service and segmentation.

The final dimension is one of geographic spread. Here again the spread is a wide one: from banks like Wachovia and Texas Commerce where international is a service function supporting domestic clients, to Citibank, a truly transnational or global bank for whom the US is simply another, albeit important, target market.

So much for profiling; the critical issue is financial performance. However one measures managerial excellence, by general consensus it should ultimately be reflected in long term financial results. For banks, the acknowledged measurement standards are return on shareholders' investment (ROI), return on assets (ROA), and growth in earnings. Quantifying this performance obliges one to cross two minefields of comparability: peer group analysis and data base.

The first obstacle can be traversed with some degree of success. Bank analysts have traditionally acknowledged the logic of peer group comparisons. Nationality, size, product range and ownership are the usual dividing lines. One can thus compare Deutsche Bank with other privately owned German banks, or better still with its peers among the 'Big Three' universal banks. Morgan and Citibank are usually compared on the basis of size with other US money centre banks, while

Sumitomo and Bank of Tokyo are ranked with the Japanese City Banks. Unique animals like the HongkongBank do not fit easily into any particular category, but by and large the analyst can rank the excellent banks by comparison with their acknowledged peers.

The trouble comes with the numbers to be used. The analyst immediately comes face to face with the classic confrontation between the Anglo-Saxon (and Scandinavian) commitment to full disclosure and the Continental European priority placed on confidence. The latter doctrine supports the build-up of hidden reserves from earnings and the under-valuation of assets so as to provide a cushion to absorb losses and produce reported data which show a steady favourable progression. The author's first job in the early 1960s as a junior American bank analyst was to determine the 'real earnings' of one of the German banks in Table 1.1. It was a totally frustrating experience then, and over twenty years later the situation has not changed materially. To quote an industry authority on the earnings of German and Swiss banks,

> The reporting rules ... permit the figures for loan loss provisions, ... exceptional capital profits and profits on 'own account' dealing ... to be recorded in such a way that management may, except in the most dire circumstances, report whatever net income it chooses. (IBCA Banking Analysis; various reports on individual banks.)

The problems posed by hidden earnings in Continental banks are compounded there and elsewhere by different views on consolidation, loan loss provisioning, devices to shelter earnings from tax and whether to include certain assets and commitments above or below the line.

Creative and persistent analysts have resorted to a variety of techniques to deal with these data limitations: the use of pre-tax figures, operating profits before trading profits or loss provisions, and capital data adjusted for certain equity-type reserves. The net result, however, is a highly imperfect one which may be adequate for peer group analysis but is hardly relevant for comparisons between peer groups.

Table 1.2 reflects these adjustments to reported data. Peer groupings and performance ratios relevant to these peer groups

TABLE 1.2 *Excellence bank financial performance by peer group*

Peer group	After tax return on equity		Pre-tax return on total assets		Pre-tax earnings growth (in %)
	1983	av. 1980–1983	1983	av. 1980–1983	1980–1983
1. *US money centre and large banks*[1]					Not relevant
Citicorp	11.66	13.16	0.52[12]	0.56[12]	93.5
Morgan	15.38	14.31	0.64[12]	0.54[12]	34.2
Bankers Trust	14.26	15.45	0.77[12]	0.71[12]	40.6
Security Pacific	15.88	17.88	0.63[12]	0.60[12]	57.5
	18.18	17.05	0.71[12]	0.68[12]	
2. *US major regional banks*[2]					Not available
Wachovia	12.48	13.04	0.74[12]	0.77[12]	79.9
Texas Commerce	18.43	14.87	1.20[12]	0.97[12]	46.7
	18.73	19.99	1.09[12]	1.12[12]	
3. *HongkongBank*	14.40	16.97	Not available		8.35[8]
4. *Major UK clearing banks*[3]					
Barclays	11.10	14.50	0.85	1.08	18.2
	11.02	16.02	0.90	1.18	6.4
5. *Major Canadian chartered banks*[4]					
Toronto Dominion	15.53	14.46	1.08	0.98	87.3
	17.78	18.68	1.50	1.42	59.3
6. *German private commercial banks*[5]	Not relevant				Not relevant[6]
Deutsche Bank	Not relevant		1.04[6]	0.70	131.3[6]
			1.22[6]	0.96[6]	

Bayerische Vereinsbank	Not relevant		0.75[6]	0.56[6]	121.0[6]
7. *Major Swiss banks*[7]					
Union Bank of Switzerland	7.08	6.63	0.57	0.57	29.9
Swiss Bank Corporation	8.90	8.06	0.72	0.72	47.6
	8.33	7.45	0.65	0.63	52.4
8. *Swedish commercial banks*[9]	Not relevant		1.64[10]	1.40[10]	123.6[10]
S-E-Banken	Not relevant		1.52[10]	1.27[10]	138.5[10]
9. *Japanese city banks*[11]	9.92	8.36	0.42	0.39	77.8
Bank of Tokyo	9.71	9.24	0.32	0.38	(9.6)
Sumitomo	13.50	11.01	0.67	0.65	65.4

[1] Keefe, Bruyette & Woods: 17 banking institutions with assets in excess of $20 billion.
[2] Keefe Bruyette & Woods: 53 banking institutions with assets between $5 billion and $20 billion.
[3] IBCA Banking Analysis: Big Four clearing banks, average data.
[4] IBCA Banking Analysis: six largest Canadian chartered banks, average data.
[5] IBCA Banking Analysis: 19 private commercial banks, average data.
[6] Pre-tax data defined as partial net operating profit (*Teilbetriebsergebnis*) before own account trading, loan loss provision, provisions to hidden reserves, etc.
[7] IBCA Banking Analysis: five major Swiss banks, average data.
[8] Net income.
[9] IBCA Banking Analysis: 14 Swedish commercial banks, average data.
[10] Net operating income before extraordinary items, allocation to 'untaxed reserves' and taxes.
[11] IBCA Banking Analysis: 13 Japanese 'city', or major banks, average data. Pre-tax profit for all Japanese banks defined as *Eigyo-Rieki* – operating profit excluding securities and special items.
[12] After tax data; pre-tax not available.

have been used to provide the best possible indication of how these banks have performed over the 1980–83 period.

What emerges from Table 1.2 is relative financial performance ranging from average to superlative. The six American excellence banks have consistently out-performed their respective peer group averages in recent years in terms of return on assets and shareholders' funds. The four larger institutions have not only demonstrated returns on equity several points above the average but also shown improved returns on assets over the 1980–83 period despite a decline for the average institution. The two regionals, Wachovia and Texas Commerce, have out-distanced their peers even more impressively with 1983 ratios at least 40 per cent higher than the average.

Outside the US, Toronto Dominion and Sumitomo have regularly been at the top of their national peer groups in recent years for most significant bottom line performance ratios. Deutsche Bank in its narrower peer group of the Big Three German universal banks has easily out-performed its rivals. The two Swiss banks and Skandinaviska Enskilda (S-E-Banken) have performed relatively well in a similar peer comparison, while Bayerische Vereinsbank's apparently sub-par performance is attributable to its unique commitment to low margin mortgage business. Barclays and Bank of Tokyo have shown average peer group results with Barclays having lost its leadership position of several years ago. Hongkong-Bank is literally in a class by itself with excellent reported results which, however, reflect European-type disclosure standards.

These impressions are confirmed by the available data provided by industry observers. The *Institutional Investor* (June 1984, p. 272), for example, ranked the world's 300 largest banks on the basis of 1983 pre-tax return on assets. Ten of the sixteen excellent banks figured in the top 100 of this listing.

It would, indeed, be splendid if presumed excellence did correlate perfectly with reported earnings performance. While this is largely true in North America and some other markets, there are a few cases where the excellent ranking given to what appear to be average performers must be attributable to other factors. Such factors might include a relatively low value placed on reported data (justifiable in several countries such as

Germany, Switzerland and Hong Kong) or anticipated improved future performance. It is clear from the above analysis that some of these banks are more excellent than others: both the financial record and our panel's voting pattern confirm this. By the same token, there is certainly no guarantee that either:

(1) these banks will continue to be relatively well managed, or that
(2) other banks do not have some or all of the same managerial qualities.

In the absence of a direct comparison with a sample of poorly performing banks, we must test our judgements in the light of the well-publicised difficulties of problem banks as well as the author's own banking and consulting experience.

The real value to be added by this book is therefore to be derived from the interview process. Through extensive and in-depth discussions with an excellent bank's top management, there should emerge patterns of management practice which are relevant to a far wider range of banks. In the last analysis, however, only when the overall mosaic becomes clear at the end of this volume can the reader decide whether these patterns are relevant for his or her bank.

To this end, up to two days were spent with a senior management team from each of the sixteen banks. The team generally included the chief executive as well as his key functional subordinates. In most instances, interviews were held with the chief credit officer, the human resources head, and senior planning and marketing officers. Discussions were off the record, but a variety of attributed and non-attributed quotations have been used in subsequent chapters to provide a much richer mosaic of managerial practice than the author's narrative ever could. There are natural limitations to the frankness with which management will respond to quite sensitive questions. On balance, however, for a half dozen independent-minded senior executives from a single bank to speak off the record to a former banker and informed observer should ensure that actual management practice is reasonably faithfully reflected.

2 Values and Culture

> *We need a framework, and it's called culture* – Bud Baker, Wachovia.

A bank's shared values constitute its culture. Such cultural values may relate to how communications take place, how decisions are made, or how people get ahead in the organisation. They are the signature, the 'what makes us different', of a bank.

The first and most overwhelming conclusion from the interview process is the strength and consistency of the values expressed by the excellent banks.

With few exceptions, shared values which penetrate throughout managerial ranks have been built up over an extended period of years. From chairman to vice-president, one hears the same litany of bonding elements – and often the same examples of their impact. Service at Wachovia, democracy at Swiss Bank Corporation, the international heritage at Bank of Tokyo and decentralisation at Citibank were the invariable responses of their senior managements to an initial query about what makes their banks unique.

The second conclusion is that these values seem to constitute or underpin the principal competitive strengths of the excellent banks. 'Hard' strengths obviously exist: principally location in one attractive market. Being based in the booming, wealthy region of Bavaria is clearly a plus for Bayerische Vereinsbank, whereas Texas Commerce is most fortunate to be in Texas. Yet, as one probes these structural strengths it is the 'soft' values which have usually enabled the bank to capitalise on hard, inherited factors such as location, secrecy legislation and special legal status. HongkongBank, for example, has been the envy of many bankers jealous of its dominant position in the highly profitable Hong Kong market. Yet in the early 1950s the bank had just lost its natural base in China and had emerged as main banker to the refugee Shanghai industrialists who had flocked to the British Territory to set up again. Hong Kong was then a far cry from its present position as one of the world's largest financial markets.

What are the values most highly prized by the excellent banks? Perhaps the first distinction to make is between financial values – principally profit – and non-financial values. *In Search of Excellence* reserves the highest praise for a value-driven company motivated by such considerations as customer service and product quality. The implication is that fulfillment of these goals, which are more easily understandable and motivating to the entire workforce, will ultimately produce a satisfactory profit performance.

For the great majority of the excellent banks, however, financial return is either the sole value or is so inextricably tied to 'soft' values that the distinction between 'profit driven' and 'value driven' is a nominal one. Most of the banks interviewed like to think of themselves as value-driven, but on closer questioning acknowledge that financial performance dominates other considerations.

For some banks, such financial values as volume growth, ROI and ROA are clearly the only shared value. Two such financially-driven banks are Texas Commerce and Bayerische Vereinsbank. To quote Marshall Tyndall, EVP-Marketing of Texas Commerce,

> **It's nebulous to talk about values. We are performance-driven; we have a much easier time defining performance objectives such as earnings growth and ROI.**

This view is echoed by a senior Bayerische Vereinsbank officer:

> **It's just a profit orientation. There's no preaching or speeches.**

Such a focus on profits in effect reflects performance as a value. Individual managers are evaluated by their peers as well as superiors on the basis of what they are perceived to bring to the bottom line.

For such banks, there is certainly an awareness of cultural values, but the dominant value in the sense of uniting the officer team is bottom-line results. As we shall discuss later, such a quantitative focus is associated with consistent leadership from the top.

Much more common is the excellent bank which articulates both financial and non-financial qualities as its shared values. The two institutions which are most committed and specific about their non-financial values are Citicorp and Wachovia.

For Citicorp, its values do not gather dust on the pages of its Annual Report: they are articulated to the questioning outsider by a variety of senior Citibankers in consistent and colourful detail.

Rick Roesch, Citicorp's SVP for Personnel Planning and Development, summarises them:

> **Integrity** – we live up to our commitments to communities and employees;
> **Customer focus** – we are totally customer driven and constantly monitor customer reactions;
> **Innovation** – we are constantly encouraging our people to be creative. And it is not enough to say 'I did something': you have also got to spread it around the organisation;
> **Decentralisation** – we have a mind set for decentralisation: we are determined to drive more decisions down to the business unit level while keeping overall control for consistency, and
> **People** – we are only as good as our people – those who strive for excellence, team-work, creativity and hard work.

To the bemused outsider who reads of such 'motherhood' qualities in countless bank publications, this constant repetition by Citibanker after Citibanker provides an awareness of the extent to which these values have permeated at least the senior management ranks of what is now the largest US bank.

John Medlin, Wachovia's chairman of the Board and CEO, describes the rationale for a value system based on financial soundness, profitability, people, products and community.

> People do pay more for excellence in the form of better service. We have come back in style from a stodgy image of the 1960s because people seem more inclined to buy quality. To many of our career employees, it is as much a dedicated mission and purposeful way of life as it is a business enterprise. Such a sense

of history, *esprit de corps* and psychic inspiration give Wachovia a subtle but real advantage in a world of fragile loyalties and elusive values.

And you have to have cultural values to pick you up. For example, we had a big problem – a courier plane went down carrying over $100 million in cheques which had to be reconstructed in a matter of days. People called from all over the organisation to offer help and eventually got the loss down to a few cents. We did not have to ask for volunteers – there is a sense of caring for each other.

What are the non-financial values which are most frequently espoused by the excellent banks?

The quality of people – often expressed as professional skills – is perhaps the foremost 'soft' value. After an introductory remark along the lines of 'we are no better than our people', the typical response opens up into a rich description of the recruiting, training, evaluation and career development process. Herewith some examples from a few of the banks generally acknowledged to have the most highly qualified bankers in the world:

Dr Wilfried Guth, member of the Board of Managing Directors of Deutsche Bank AG, points out that:

> We are oriented towards profitability, but our number one value is the quality of our people. There is no specific miracle drug, but we at the *Vorstand* level spend a great deal of time on careful personnel career planning, going over long lists of candidates, to be as sure as possible of making the right choice.

Virtually the same thoughts are expressed by Lewis Preston, Morgan's chairman:

> What distinguishes the bank starts at the recruiting phase, where senior management meets the trainees. Career path planning – moving people around – is critical to obtain not just commercial bankers but financiers.

And Walter Wriston, former chairman of Citicorp:

> Year in year out, we recruit, train and motivate the very best men and women we can find in the world.

Another perspective on the human resource issue is obtained by noting the frequency with which the excellent banks express concern about the availability of sufficient qualified people in the future. It is somewhat unnerving to ask all three banks – Citicorp, Deutsche, and Morgan – heading up the excellent list of their principal concern for the future and to be told it is just that: availability of the right people.

To quote Citicorp's Roesch,

> We've got the deepest bench [of talent] statistically, but it's not enough. Our new businesses consume more manpower than expected – it's the flagellation that keeps you going.

He is echoed by Dr Guth of Deutsche Bank:

> We have a continous demand for good people. When it comes to sudden needs, for example in new fields of financial activity, we still have to struggle to find sufficiently skilled staff.

For Morgan's EVP of Administration, Bruce Brackenridge, the problem for the future is:

> We do not hire enough of the most exceptional people – the top 20 per cent of the MBAs. We need to manage the change from a relationship to a transaction banker.

The human resource development process and the steps banks are taking to meet these needs will be discussed in Chapter 8.

A second common value is the openness or democracy of an excellent bank's culture. These banks tend to be permeated by total communication – both vertically and horizontally – whether they are high-pressure institutions like Deutsche or Citicorp or relatively relaxed ones like Morgan and Bank of Tokyo. Texas Commerce and Bayerische Vereinsbank are renowned for their strong top-down leadership, yet senior officers at both speak of 'over-communication' and strong consultation by the CEO with his subordinates.

Such openness can be appreciated best by talking to people at the working level who have frequent access to the top executive team. Listen to a VP at Toronto Dominion:

> **Rank is not a factor in our relationship. The other day I was talking to the CEO on the telephone while the President was on the line to talk to me.**

And a SVP in the same bank:

> **There is a degree of informality in the executive suite. We never find the time to respect the pecking order – we just get the job done.**

Even in the more highly structured, hierarchical banks, the vertical communications channels are open. In the Bank of Tokyo, the traditional ranking based on seniority is softened by good communications wherein personal names tend to be used rather than the individual's title, as is usual in Japanese banks. 'Freedom of speech' is a phrase heard often at Swiss Bank Corporation, Citicorp and Deutsche Bank. Chairman Franz Galliker of Swiss Bank Corporation, which prides itself on its Swiss Federalist democracy with seven equal members of the Executive Committee, talks of 'open doors'. The Management Board structure of Swiss, German and Japanese banks ensures daily, often intense, interaction between top management and bankers at the operating level. A friend at Deutsche Bank says:

> **Things are unbelievably free. We have lots of committees and meetings up and down the organisation. I can talk to other departments and initiate ideas. And I have never worked so hard in my life.**

A characteristic of this open culture is a strong informal decision-making process. At Texas Commerce, it is called 'hall-way decisions', which supplement the extensive use of committees. At the Japanese banks, the famous bottom-up consensus rules. And losing an argument is not a fatal blow. As Toronto Dominion's Chairman, Dick Thomson, says

Its not a big event here to get overruled. You say what you think.

In the Continental European and Japanese banks, a matrix structure at the top fosters – and effectively requires – such an openness and high level of communication. The need for consensus – if not unanimity – from perhaps a dozen top managers who have both geographic and functional responsibilities demands a high level of interaction involving subordinates as well as Management Board members. At the staff level, a Deutsche Bank international area head describes the communication process:

> **When we discuss a country limit proposal, we get together all the relevant staff and line departments and have a deep and rather intensive discussion to come up with our recommendations to the *Vorstand*. It takes time, but we hate to go to them with two opinions – that's rare.**

At the Management Board level itself, where Deutsche Bank prides itself on having unanimous agreement among twelve strong and often outspoken members, Dr Eckard Van Hooven describes the process:

> **We have to use very clear discipline in expressing our wishes; if not, the results could be disastrous. We must consider the interests of our partners. It may take longer than if we have one chief, but we get better bottom-line results because we have thoroughly discussed the issue. Brick-by-brick we build the discussion – and out of nothing the decision is there.**

A friend at Sumitomo Bank describes the intense formal and informal communications process there:

> **Our communications are quite excellent. When McKinsey studied us, they had nothing to criticize in this respect. The problem is perhaps the reverse – it's a real cost. Each group head is a member of the Executive Committee, which meets twice a week for about two hours. Its incredible.**

At the Swiss Bank Corporation, a senior staff officer relates the communications process in connection with an asset/

liability group meeting:

> Our top management makes unanimous decisions. The style works well: it's based on an understanding of the people involved. Even the strong-minded men – and we have them – accept the process of letting people be part of the decision. It is almost a debating club but casual and more effective. The dialogue melts into a consensus.

In the excellent US banks, communication is the standard rather than the exception. The respected Morgan culture relies on it. Rodney Wagner, the Vice-Chairman of Morgan's Credit Policy Committee, talks of:

> an informal, open culture. We have all sorts of rules and regulations, but it does not really mean much on a day-to-day basis. Lew Preston's door is open.

Another Morgan friend speaks of Morgan's being

> quite a pleasant place to work, with a certain ease to relationships, a high level of mutual respect, not much politics and an astonishing amount of support given to the individual. We are a value-driven organisation with a collegial, deliberative decision-making process. We automatically start consulting with each other.

Morgan's Brackenridge sums up:

> The organisation works more by consensus than others. It takes a long time to make decisions, but they are well thought out. Word of mouth is part of our soft culture. If there is a problem, we just sit down and knock it out.

Morgan's culture seen from the outside is viewed with some respect. Says Citicorp's chief lending officer, Larry Glenn:

> Morgan is extraordinary. It is totally consensual; but I hear even they are finally finding it necessary to put it in writing and install controls.

Security Pacific is another excellent US bank which prides itself on its open management culture. The culture stems in large part from the relaxed California environment as well as a senior management group which has grown up together in the retail arm of the institution and has established a high level of mutual trust. At Texas Commerce, openness takes the form of a committee structure in which management as well as credit decisions are discussed and communicated.

A corollary of this open communication in the excellent banks is what is usually described as a family feeling. At Toronto Dominion, senior credit officer Ted McDowell describes

> ... a family feeling. People who work for Toronto Dominion get a lot of green paint [the bank's colour] in their blood.

This bond of career kinship carries with it a variety of assumptions: communication, trust, support in times of personal stress, and the implicit assumption that a job will be available as long as the family member plays the game by the rules. A senior non-Swiss executive of Swiss Bank Corporation looks back on his career with the bank:

> Personal ties get very, very close. They build tremendous loyalty. Firing people in my area was a federal case; the Chairman wanted to save people. But you've got to play the game.

In the Far East and some Continental European countries, the family feeling is part and parcel of a lifetime employment tradition. At Swiss Bank Corporation, a senior staff officer characterises it as follows:

> The bank tries to find the right place for everyone. There is a feeling of belonging and a high level of trust in the man on the line. If he has a problem, we find him a place.

Time after time, in banks like Toronto Dominion one hears the phrase 'we make it hard for people to fail in this bank'. The family analogy is carried one step further by a Citibank SVP in discussing the innovation process:

It is like a Jewish family: we all argue, squabble and come up with new ideas. People here feel strongly; it's part of the culture.

An open environment clearly plays a critical role in the process of conflict resolution in the decision-making process. However long the process takes in a bank like Swiss Bank Corporation or Deutsche Bank, all relevant views are heard, the issues belaboured, and a decision is made to which all positively subscribe. Deutsche Bank's Van Hooven describes his semi-annual, two-day strategy meeting with the regional personal banking heads known in the bank as his praetorian guard:

For the first half day, the flood gates are open – everybody gets things off his chest. Then we study the proposals, make a target agreement and march off together.

In similar vein, Morgan's Brackenridge talks about some suggested changes in the bank's training programme:

We sent a questionnaire to about 800 people in the bank to get their views. It will be discussed *ad nauseam* – to the point of boredom. But it will bring the issues out.

A third value of many of the excellent banks is their heritage. Virtually every bank has its heroes, its war stories, its founding fathers and the tale of its genesis. The interviewer is usually given a generous dose of history before a response is given to a specific question about current management practices. This managerial mind set reflects a cultural framework which provides strength and guidance, particularly in a large, far-flung banking operation. Since banking has changed little since the days of the relevant founding father, his precepts are often applied in the 1980s with some degree of relevance.

The names of Jesse Jones of Texas Commerce, Robert Hanes of Wachovia, the Osaka merchants of 300 years ago who established Sumitomo Bank, the old Yokohama Specie Bank which antedated the Bank of Tokyo, the Quaker families who set up Barclays' predecessors in the nineteenth century – all are brought quickly to mind by today's managers as they address current management issues. It can be more implicit: just as

Morgan does not put its name on the door at 23 Wall Street in New York, one does not need to ask the name of the fierce gentleman with a prominent nose in the portraits that decorate so many Morgan offices.

The traditions established by these founding fathers or more recent heroes are equally powerful in the value structure of these excellent banks. Strong leaders such as Baron von Tucher of Bayerische Vereinsbank, Hermann Abs of Deutsche Bank and Walter Wriston of Citibank have placed an indelible stamp on their successors' views of the world. For these banks such leadership itself can be a cultural value. The tradition of the profit-minded Osaka merchants (who are reputed to greet each other by saying 'how much money did you make today') is contrasted in today's Sumitomo Bank with the more effete traditions of its Tokyo-based competitors. A few blocks away at the Bank of Tokyo, today's managers continue the pioneering international tradition of foreign exchange and trade finance inaugurated by its predecessor institution.

The presence of descendants of the founding families of Barclays in its current management structure is viewed as a positive value. At HongkongBank, Deputy Chairman Willie Purves describes the impact of the bank's heritage:

> **It was set up by local merchants in Hong Kong, since the local branches at the time faced delays in getting approvals from London head office by sea mail. We have tried to keep it that way ever since by delegating more authority to our branch managers than almost anyone else. Our local people are in charge of everything that goes on in their markets.**

Perhaps the most vivid use of heritage as a contemporary value is seen at Wachovia. New trainees are greeted by a film describing the bank's 105 year history as well as a talk by CEO Medlin on the values espoused by his predecessors. The picture of one of the latter, with appropriate credit aphorisms, actually hangs in the office of Wachovia's chief credit officer, Bud Baker. As Baker explains,

> **Hokey it may seem, but it is needed. We need a framework, and its called culture. Banking has not changed much since his day; bells and whistles have come and gone. John Medlin and I visit**

all the credit training programmes; it is like dusting off the tablets.

A related value is a widespread tradition among the excellent banks of growing their own talent in the form of people who join the bank after high school or university for a lifetime career. With few exceptions, it is a badge of honour for these banks to provide both general bankers and specialists from their own ranks. To quote Dr Nikolaus Senn, President of the Executive Board of the Union Bank of Switzerland:

> **We grow our own. Sometimes we have to take people from outside for technical or international jobs, but I consider it poor performance if we can not use our own people.**

This view is echoed at HongkongBank, Bank of Tokyo, Deutsche Bank and a variety of others. Swiss Bank Corporation has recruited several senior foreigners to head up major overseas units; as a friend there explains:

> **they fit in with the Swiss Bank style – conservative, prudent and humane.**

The corollary of this home-grown culture is often a distinct feeling of unease on the part of the outsider – usually staff specialists or foreigners – who join in mid-career. Such a senior HongkongBank manager describes it as 'being an outsider in a club atmosphere'.

Another value common to a large number of excellent banks is a commitment to delegation or decentralisation. Sometimes, as at Citicorp, it is a conscious decision consistent with a commitment to strategic management and the firm belief that a large, multinational, multi-product bank can not be effectively managed except on such a basis. Jack Heilshorn, Citibank's EVP for Corporate Strategy, attributes this commitment to Citibank's managerial culture:

> **Our commitment to decentralisation follows from ours being a people business. It's all built around our major preoccupation to recruit the best and the brightest people who can plant flags around the world and make their own decisions. And we really**

believe that the best place to make decisions is as close to the customer as you can get.

For most other banks, decentralisation is a historical tradition which has proved its value. Deutsche Bank has consciously built up the importance of its fourteen regional head branches in Germany who in turn supervise the smaller units in their territories. It is the conflicts between these profit centres and the central staff which provide much of the fodder for discussion at Board level. Similarly, Swiss Bank Corporation has retained the 'federalist' autonomy of its seventeen major Swiss branches, each of which retains its own full-service capabilities. Overseas correspondent banking relationships and international money market dealings, however, are concentrated with the main offices in Basle, Zurich and Geneva.

S-E-Banken has both a material and historical rationale for its heritage of regional decentralisation. Chairman Curt G. Olsson describes the merger process which produced strong units in the regional centres of Malmoe and Göteborg:

> Our market share overall in Sweden is about 24 per cent, but we have about 40 per cent of each of these markets as a result of the 1971 merger. We need to be seen to have a final decision-maker in each city.

For HongkongBank, historical traditions of decentralisation are reinforced by the competitive advantage of quick credit response time. Deputy Chairman Purves feels that local knowledge and mutual trust permit

> a credit process, based on personal lending limits, which our competitors cannot meet in terms of fast decisions. With people who have been in the bank up to thirty years you can pick up the telephone and talk to someone who trusts you.

In the world of British clearing banks, known for a slow-moving, pyramidal decision-making process, Barclays regards itself as unique for its decentralised management style. General Manager Richard Carden attributes this to

> a historical feature going back to the series of partnerships which, when they amalgamated into Barclays, kept local part-

ners to run their area. We call them Local Directors now, with line responsibility for about eighty branches each. They are still independent-minded: head office spins out instructions in circulars, but the Local Directors use their discretion.

A final characteristic of most excellent banks is that management works very, very, hard. The pressure to perform is often reinforced by wide spans of control and lean staffs, which are discussed in Chapter 6. Frequent task-force assignments in banks like Toronto Dominion and Bank of Tokyo are simply added to normal line assignments. Open communication means lots of meetings in addition to the tasks of getting the work and keeping close to the customer. Even in workaholic Hong Kong, the HongkongBank stands out, as a senior staffer explains:

We have grown five-fold in balance sheet terms in six years. The overstretch on executives is enormous. Manpower is a serious restraint.

At Toronto Dominion, one hears the same from a senior lending officer:

Our principal weakness? Our lean approach is a double-edged sword. Internal promotion is OK but we have not got a deep bench.

Not all of the excellent banks, by any stretch of the imagination, possess all of these positive bonds. Perhaps only Citicorp does to any significant extent. Yet what characterises all of the values described above is consistency: years and years of focus on one or more elements which bind together thousands of people often scattered in dozens of countries around the world. There have not been radical changes of direction, even though leadership may have changed frequently. Such a consistent cultural pattern must represent a significant potential bond for individual managers in a complex world populated by hundreds of competitors selling roughly the same products to the same client base. How useful the bond of common values is will be discussed in subsequent chapters.

There are, however, one or two excellent banks that have

recently undertaken such a radical cultural change. Bankers Trust and, to a lesser extent, Security Pacific have embarked on courses which are taking them far from their cultural base of the mid-1970s. Evaluating their strategic rationale – to become a merchant bank in the case of Bankers Trust and a broadly-based financial services firm in that of Security Pacific – is beyond the scope of this book, but their experiences in changing values is of central importance to bank management everywhere. The forces for change in banking are obliging many excellent banks to review their strategies, with major cultural and other implications. The case study of Bankers Trust is thus a fascinating laboratory test for cultural change.

George Vojta, Bankers Trust's EVP for Strategic Planning, summarises the bank's new value system:

> **Bankers Trust is value-driven: the driving value is a code word – merchant banking – which is a way of doing business. This emerging force is becoming embedded in the hearts and minds of our people. Involving people requires constant interaction and reinforcement; it is cumulative and gradual. You cannot short-circuit the time span – it takes years. There is no substitute for face-to-face communications.**

The essential change is one faced by many commercial banks: to move from a relationship-based structure focused on building assets and loan volume to one tied to money and capital markets where transactions and risk positioning are key. Bankers Trust's David Beim, whose Corporate Finance function is at the centre of this process of change, explains that:

> **Market values are now critical: this implies volatility and a sense of urgency. We are not selling entertainment any more and we do not need a socialist culture. Culture becomes more tense because of the fast pace of capital and money markets.**

Changing direction towards its new definition of merchant banking has involved divestiture of retail and other units as well as the departure – voluntary and otherwise – of a number of traditional commercial bankers. The chief executive is at the centre of the process of cultural change. Bankers Trust's

Alfred Brittain III describes his philosophy:

> We changed direction from a product-for-every-market General Motors: we sold the Chevvy and focused on the Cadillac Division. In the 1970s, unit profitabiliy was the key: there wasn't an emphasis on people helping each other. Now we need a common-purpose culture for Bankers Trust. Our value now is excellence through common purpose.

Security Pacific is another excellent bank which has gone through a certain amount of cultural change as it diversifies away from a regional focus on California-based retail and corporate banking to a wide range of non-bank financial services around the world. The challenge is to retain but restructure the bank's traditional strong base in California, yet develop new activities through acquisition. Security Pacific is one of only two excellent institutions to have relied extensively in recent years on growth through acquisition. The others prefer to grow new businesses internally just as they grow their own people. The second excellent bank to grow recently by acquisition, HongkongBank, has avoided cultural change through its strict policy of local autonomy.

From the standpoint of cultural values, the challenge for Security Pacific is to mesh its inbred, open culture with the new emphasis on entrepreneurial drive, performance measurement, and specialist skills brought in from the outside. As EVP Irving Margol, SecPac's head of Management Services, describes the current position:

> With our goal of creating a balanced, diversified financial institution, we have a more competitive culture than ever before. We need co-operation to get lower costs and higher quality. Flexibility is the name of the game. We have put trust department people out in the branch system. Some of them have never been inside a branch before. They are no longer in the Taj Mahal. But this is the world we're dealing with. We say to them: if you are not happy, we either retrain you or work out a settlement with you.

SecPac's Vice-Chairman Robert Smith, who has responsibility for its fast-moving capital markets group, argues for autonomy for his capital markets activities:

> They run well and grow fast with specialised industry management operating outside the culture of the more traditional banking functions.

SecPac's strong in-group culture may suffer from the infusion of new professionals and the pressure to perform. Its Vice-Chairman with responsibility for the California Banking Office System, Roy Hartmann, acknowledges this:

> Our strength as a close-knit organisation is that we can talk the same language five levels down the organisation so that we all understand what top management wants. Our great strength at SecPac is our capacity to execute, which is 90 per cent of the battle. But this inbred culture can be a weakness as we bring professionals into new, specialised businesses.

Changing one's cultural values is one response to the evolving requirements of the market-place. Another is to develop multiple cultures. Several of the excellent banks acknowledge the existence of different cultures within their organisations and attempt to reinforce these opposing values rather than go through the top-to-bottom change under way at Bankers Trust. Such a view is perhaps best expressed at S-E-Banken, whose commitment to decentralisation could facilitate such compartmentalisation. Here is how Jacob Palmstierna, Managing Director of SEB, articulates the philosophy:

> The only way to develop an investment banking capability is to have separate cultures, which is why we set up Enskilda Securities in London with a 30 per cent minority interest for management. You must be open to create different cultures which compete among each other. 'We and they' is a risk, but we are convinced that a successful specialist operation requires taking it. We all cannot sing together; we have to accept that each branch has a little bit of its own culture.

Chairman Olsson agrees but acknowledges the need to try to bridge the gap:

We would like to spin more operations off with subsidiaries with a Managing Director more directly responsible and a profit and loss statement to let them create their own culture. But we also have a problem with the antagonism between retail and corporate banking. Retail has an inferiority complex; it is a challenge to get people to understand how interdependent things are. We need to build up their self-confidence.

Having acknowledged the existence of different cultures, S-E-Banken has established a 'shared values' committee among its employees to determine what can be done to improve commitment to the bank. Chairman Olsson's hope is to win the hearts and minds of the minority which constitutes the opinion-makers among the employees.

Another excellent bank moving in the same direction as S-E-Banken is Barclays. Having acquired a stockbroker and jobber in anticipation of the restructuring of the London Stock Exchange, Barclays will be giving up a 25 per cent interest in its new stock exchange affiliate to management.

Acknowledges General Manager Carden:

Obviously different skills are needed in this business, and it won't be fully institutionalised. It is a bold move for Barclays.

The excellent banks thus do have strong values which have been reinforced over an extended period of time. Their importance is reflected in Bankers Trust's efforts to cultivate new ones which management feels are more appropriate in the prospective market environment for banks. How relevant are an open culture, a strong heritage, decentralisation and a focus on people?

Based on the experience of the excellence banks, it is hard to quarrel with the positive contribution each of these values can make. Values themselves, of course, do not produce bottom-line profits, but the experience of these banks is that they definitely provide an environment in which profits are easier to make. The physical size and complexity of most of the excellent banks – assuming proper central controls and guidance – argues strongly for decentralisation. An open culture aids in conflict resolution and improves communications. A strong heritage provides a rallying point, a support framework, and often some quite useful operating guidelines for today's practitioners.

As for people as a value, the issue is not its relevance but rather the negative implications of a homogeneous culture. Growing up together in an institution fosters trust – a vital factor in credit and other decisions – as well as communications and a personal support mechanism. But it has its obvious negative connotations of lack of experience outside the bank, resistance to change and opposition to newcomers who might make a useful contribution. These issues will be evaluated in Chapter 8.

3 Strategic Direction

The best planning is done as close to the customer as you can get – Jack Heilshorn, Citibank

The strategic planning process for a bank serves as a long-term directional goal, a framework for action and a means of monitoring progress in achieving targets. It involves major choices, the setting of priorities, the allocation of resources and the identifying of responsibilities.

This chapter has been devoted to strategic direction as a means of linking the values discussed previously with a market-oriented plan of action. In a word, do the excellent banks think strategically, and what techniques do they employ in planning and implementing such forward thinking?

At first, there are almost as many responses to this question as there are excellent banks. The apparent profusion of responses, however, seems to reflect a few key variables:

(1) *External pressure for change*. There is a fairly high degree of correlation between banks facing major profit constraints in their core businesses and the willingness to commit themselves seriously to a strategic plan.
(2) *Willingness of top management to accept change*. The strength of the planning commitment is invariably a function of the chief executive's interest in the process. In the absence of this commitment, there are some rather frustrated staff planners, even among the excellent banks.
(3) *Phase on the planning life-cycle*. Having made a serious commitment to the strategic planning process to achieve change, excellent bank management often produces at that point a major medium-term strategic framework which is followed in subsequent years by decentralised, shorter-terms plans within the longer-term framework.

An examination of the planning process of most excellent institutions thus reflects in effect a three-phase life-cycle:

(1) Management initially sees no need to commit itself to change through a strategic effort;
(2) External pressures force management to make strategic choices, and a long-term action plan is established;
(3) A framework having been established for planning, responsibility is delegated to individual business units, with a small central planning staff co-ordinating the plans of these units to minimise paperwork. Planning then becomes 'middle up and middle down'.

At one end of this cycle are the banks that perceive little or no real threat to their basic businesses. These banks tend to have profitable shares of growing core markets. For Texas Commerce and Bayerische Vereinsbank, therefore, planning essentially involves financial projections reflecting continued volume and profit growth in traditional businesses over the short and possibly medium term. The confidence which underpins such a process is reflected in the following succinct strategy statement by a senior Bayerische Vereinsbank officer:

> **We have a very strong regional retail base so that we can afford to be a wholesale bank internationally. We have few economic problems; it's just good luck and the confidence that comes from a strong hidden reserve position. There is no strategic plan, but we do look at long-run scenarios with the Board from time to time.**

At HongkongBank, Deutsche Bank and Morgan Guaranty, strategic planning takes the form of periodic discussions between top management and the planning staff which result in issue papers relating to acquisitions, capital adequacy, a redirection of asset or liability policy and other discrete issues. They often take the form of 'what if' sensitivity exercises tied to variables such as loan volume, funding and economic growth. At Morgan, for example, SVP Robert McKeracher outlines the strategic planning process:

> **Once a year in September the top management team goes through strategic issues such as funding, acquisitions and structure, and planning papers are written. Six months later there is a follow-up in the form of a two-to-three page paper on corporate**

direction communicated to all officers to give them an idea of where the bank is going. We do not find a standard, five-year frame useful.

For the two German excellent banks, strategic planning takes the form of scenarios or what Deutsche Bank calls 'optimisation exercises'.

Most of the excellent banks have a small formal or informal strategic planning team of top management officers and perhaps a senior planner who hold brainstorming exercises and direct the strategic planning effort. At HongkongBank it is the *ad hoc* committee comprising the chairman, deputy chairman and head of strategic planning. At Deutsche Bank it is a Management Board offshoot called the 'co-ordinating group for strategic questions' which prepares options for the Board's consideration. For these banks, a formal long-term planning process is considered unrealistic and unproductive.

For another group of excellent banks, however, a longer term format is viewed as more appropriate. Such a process may reflect an effort on the part of the planning staff to encourage top management to think strategically. At Swiss Bank Corporation, for example, there has been a greater focus on top-down planning with the Board setting long term targets. As the bank's Executive Director in charge of planning points out, however,

We do not rule out goals suggested by the front line people.

A senior Swiss Bank Corporation planning officer concurs:

You can't stick a tag on this bank with regard to goals. Each drive is counterbalanced by an opposite drive. It's healthy, but it makes strategic planning a tedious affair. There is an extremely broad feeling of mission relating to client satisfaction.

For most banks with such a medium-term planning focus, goals are composed of a mix of market share, volume and profit targets. A bank like S-E-Banken aims at retaining its predominant physical position in the Nordic world and achieving key capitalisation and profit targets. Union Bank of Switzerland's chief executive is convinced of the necessity for medium-term planning but insists on 'simplicity and clarity'.

Sumitomo's strategic planning process is designed to create a 'world-class institution'. As a friend at the bank points out,

> **It's not Japanese to have explicit goals. Setting such an imprecise target gives us room to interpret it in different ways.**

In some cases, strategic planning is initiated to deal with a perceived need for change. The Bank of Tokyo in 1981 thus assigned a director to strengthen a three-year plan looking at the future of banking and designing an action plan for the bank.

Tamotsu Yamaguchi, who carried out the assignment, summarises his findings:

> **There are a lot of obstacles to change. We decided that increasing profit was our goal – our *only* goal. We identified five product groups to which we should transfer resources. There was a lot of interaction with the Management Board; they had never had this type of discussion before. We had had thirty divisions at Tokyo headquarters; we reorganised them into four groups, each with a head who has profit responsibility.**

For a bank that had traditionally regarded itself as a special institution acting almost as a arm of the Japanese Ministry of Finance, such a focus on profits and profit responsibility has been a major change. Conversations with other Bank of Tokyo officers reflect the continued importance to some of them of these traditional non-financial objectives.

Finally, there are excellent banks who plan strategically in the sense of delegating planning responsibility to business units operating within a framework of goals agreed in the past through an intensive strategic review process. In such a bank, the central planning function is reduced to a co-ordinating role with, in many cases, the chief executive himself functioning as the senior planning officer.

Perhaps the archetype of this strategic planning concept is Citicorp.

Jack Heilshorn provides the rationale:

Our commitment to decentralisation means that the best planning is done as close to the customer as you can get. I used to be chief of Walt Wriston's staff – we had 120 people there – now we have only two for the entire planning function at corporate level. What drives the organisation is the annual operating plan. We used to fill file cabinets full of long-range plans but kept changing them. Now, each business does its own planning – it can be long term or short term. I preoccupy myself with corporate strategy and business linkage.

Other excellent banks echo a disillusionment with heavy top-down, paper-intensive long range planning. S-E-Banken's Olsson points out that:

We used to have a strategic planning department, but we are not convinced this is the way. We put more emphasis on functional, annual planning by the Managing Directors of our five units.

George Vojta, Bankers Trust's planning head, describes the life-cycle of strategic planning in major US banks:

In the 1970s, we had a MIS environment – one of the major ingestions from Corporate America. But it spawned a huge bureaucracy – a twelve month permanent experience – and has reached the point where it is disfunctional. The emphasis now is on simplification. In investment banks, controls flow from people's heads; in commercial banking, from management processes. Salomon Brothers has a set of doctrines which govern behaviour without planning and provide control incentives and good profits.

A similar philosophy is expressed by the chief executives of Toronto Dominion and Wachovia. John Medlin says:

Each group has its own plan; it's bottom up and top down for each business. I'm the overall planner and bring it all together. It's impressionistic, not a detailed model. I try to make my colleagues think strategically – you keep repeating objectives to change their behaviour.

The outsider thus finds a wide range of attitudes towards establishing and implementing a strategic course of action. This range seems to reflect top management's views on two essential points: awareness of the need for change, and willingness to become involved personally in the strategic process. Understandably, banks like Bayerische Vereinsbank and Texas Commerce with highly profitable and growing core markets may not see the need for a significant change of direction. Conversely, Bankers Trust and Citibank without such a franchise have been prepared to devote the necessary resources to strategic change.

The other variable is the priority placed on strategic planning by the chief executive. Any form of planning in a large, multinational, multi-product and multi-client organisation is bound to be a highly time- and paper-consuming exercise. Without the knowledge that the chief executive is solidly behind the enterprise, it can also become a seemingly pointless one to the staff who must do the work. Even more important is the leadership contribution of the chief executive who himself plays the role of chief planning officer and can therefore impart his personal perspective to the process.

An interesting sidelight is the rarity of a mission statement among the excellent banks. Mission statements, which are designed to profile a bank to its own staff and the outside world, summarise the goals, personality and style of a particular institution. A related technique is establishing a superordinate goal – a sort of corporate battle cry – which hopefully unites bank staff and distinguishes the bank in the minds of its clients from the proliferation of competitors.

With few exceptions, the excellent banks do not have much time for corporate battle cries or mission statements. The mission statements of Wachovia, Citi and Barclays are relatively unique as is Bankers Trust's merchant banking battle cry or superordinate goal. Wachovia's reads as follows:

To serve in a fair, balanced and exemplary manner the interests of shareholders, customers, employees and the public through adherence to high standards of financial soundness, customer service, employee professionalism, business ethics, corporate citizenship and profitability.

Many banks have an implicit, understood feeling as to who they are, but it is not articulated in a few words to all and sundry. The internal and external view of Morgan, for example, is a reasonably well defined one of a prestigious, quality institution which, in the old J. P. Morgan tradition, does business only with the best people in a first-class way. Bankers in a variety of excellent institutions describe themselves as being in the Morgan mould. Yet Morgan itself finds it unnecessary to distill this image into a superordinate goal or mission statement beyond a statement in its 1983 Annual Report referring to the three basic principles of capital strength, profitability, and offering sophisticated financial services.

On the contrary, most excellent banks deprecate the idea. At Morgan itself, one planner calls a mission statement 'a fight song without the music'. A senior HongkongBank banker thinks he would be greeted 'with mirth and merriment' if he suggested such a statement to his chief executive. Many others are considering the idea but have clearly not found a positive echo among their colleagues.

One obvious explanation is that the excellent banks, having become so, do not need to spread the word. It is for lesser mortals, those struggling for recognition, who need to disseminate their message. True enough, but one is still impressed by the focus of the excellent banks on *being* excellent rather than telling the world about it.

One should not underestimate, however, the energy devoted to planning on the part of excellent banks committed to a planning goal. Toronto Dominion has eschewed a mission statement and, according to CEO Thomson,

> **dislikes policies – dumb decisions are made because of policies.**

The annual planning process there, however, is terrifying in its rigour. Comptroller Norman Roth describes a planning dialogue on a branch by branch, product by product basis for TD's 1000-odd branches:

> **We use numbers to challenge costs – its a challenging, not threatening atmosphere. In some cases, we make four passes to arrive at an acceptable plan – we figure that's enough!**

Adds President Robin Korthals,

> We try to get people to feel they can influence the numbers; perhaps only half think they can, but that's better than the competition. People will ignore 80 per cent of what they are told, but we focus on a different 20 per cent every year.

4 Products: Diversification and Innovation

> *We're 'aggressively conservative' with a lot of checks and balances* – DuWayne Peterson, Security Pacific

The banking sector has been viewed from both the outside and inside as having enjoyed – or suffered – a much more stable product range than most comparable service industries. The two traditional core businesses of banking have been the taking of deposits, which has led to banks' dominating most national payments systems around the world, and the extension of credit in a variety of forms. Most banks have expanded into related activities: the trading of currencies and securities as an adjunct to their role as a principal investor; the management and custody of third party funds, and the sale of financial advice in various forms. Where no legal barriers exist, they have expanded as 'universal' banks into – and usually come to dominate – the local securities sector as underwriter, trader, adviser and principal.

Whether universal or not, banks have been facing increasing and well publicised competitive pressure in both of their core businesses. The defection of creditworthy borrowers to cheaper sources of funds (and, as depositors, to more reliable homes for their surplus funds); the deregulation of deposit markets; competition from non-bank institutions – all have focused bankers' attention on the merits of broadening their product base either by co-opting existing or innovating new products.

If taking deposits and on-lending them are not very rewarding especially given regulators' growing concern for capital adequacy, how should the banks react? By simply moving into related but existing products, such as stockbroking, securities underwriting or life insurance, are they not simply increasing competition in already mature fields where they have no particular expertise?

Perhaps more importantly, can banks innovate in the sense of gaining a significant competitive advantage by developing new products? A broad range of insiders as well as outsider observers thinks not. Yet *In Search of Excellence* equates an innovative capability with excellence. Does this mean banks are beyond the pale?

The thrust of this chapter will therefore be to examine the record of the excellent banks in successfully broadening their product range. The emphasis will be on expansion through innovation rather than simply co-opting existing products from a competitor. And if these banks *have* successfully innovated, what techniques and practices have they employed?

The evidence shows, once again, a wide range of responses. At one extreme are several excellent banks who see no particular point in investing in innovation. For them, if a product has proved its worth, they will add it to their range, but there is no point in up-front investment to obtain a leadership position. To quote Dr Senn of Union Bank of Switzerland:

> We are in all the businesses and we have an innovative team. But banking won't change drastically. There's no new pill coming. Innovation is having good people.

Security Pacific, Texas Commerce, Bayerische Vereinsbank and a variety of others emphasise their preference for entering a product area after the bugs of the new product have been worked out and it has proved its worth. A senior Texas Commerce staff officer feels the bank has other priorities:

> I make a lot of recommendations to our long-range strategy committee, but our focus is geographic, not product expansion. We are not very interested in new products; discount brokerage looks interesting but as a defensive step. Our real opportunity is increasing our present 15 per cent share of the Texas lending market.

Security Pacific is investing substantial amounts in automating and segmenting its branch administration. Yet DuWayne Peterson, head of its automation subsidiary, points out that:

We're 'aggressively conservative' with a lot of checks and balances. As a result we were almost last in California to introduce ATMs. We prefer to let someone else test the market, then move in to take market share. There isn't a bias towards action as at IBM.

Another group of excellent banks acknowledges that being first is not necessarily essential, but they are still committed to investing in new products. Wachovia emphasises a focus on selective innovation in critical product areas. CEO Medlin describes his approach:

> In some things we do not want to be first, but it's different if we see more fundamental change. In the late 1960s, we felt we had to find a speciality in the national corporate market and picked cash management to spearhead our move. This involved developing an exceptional operating capability, but we got into lots of relationships as a result. In 1971 we began a long term strategic programme in retail banking. We did a big survey to find out what customers wanted and were told that they wanted to talk to a person, not a machine, so we developed the concept of the Personal Banker – a person to talk to, the umbilical cord to the customer. In a word, we look for big changes and make big investments in them.

Another excellent bank which has innovated selectively is Morgan. With a limited client base for which it competes with the US investment banks, Morgan has developed a competitive advantage by its pioneering role in interest rate and currency swaps. These arbitrage products are particularly appropriate for a bank with strong corporate contacts and a worldwide geographic spread, but Morgan's good internal communications and high calibre of personnel have also been essential. Morgan's London-based subsidiary, Morgan Guaranty Ltd, has used this competitive advantage to become a leader in the highly competitive Euro-bond market. Chairman Preston's priorities therefore include:

> Developing these value-added skills and integrating them into our banking business. The objective is for the line banker to develop in the natural course of things a knowledge of these transactions so *he* can present the idea to the next client.

Perhaps the most interesting aspect of this innovative leap forward is that Morgan, as pointed out earlier, is a highly reflective organisation with a strong consensual decision-making process.

Another pattern of product development is that of the Japanese excellent banks. The process of differentiation in Japan must be regarded in the context of the national culture. As a senior Japanese banker explains to a Western observer:

> **Japanese have a mentality based on relative, not absolute values. You may be the only virtuous member of your community, but you being different makes you wrong: it's the culture of shame. In Japanese banking, therefore, one wants to be seen to be only *marginally* better than the rest. True happiness is having an excuse to be better, and Sumitomo, which is from Osaka rather than Tokyo, and Bank of Tokyo, which is the 'foreign exchange bank', have that excuse.**

In product development, however, innovation does not come easily even to the two excellent Japanese banks. Perhaps reflecting this Japanese trait, a friend at Sumitomo describes innovation at his bank:

> **It's a tough question. The big Japanese banks try to be innovative, but the results are not very different. We have maybe been ahead by a few inches because of our corporate style. To use an analogy, if dry is the aggressive US style and wet is the Japanese approach with a total seniority system and no performance evaluation, we're a bit more dry than wet. I'm not satisfied with our performance on new products. If we are doing better than other Japanese banks, they are too slow.**

Dealing with new products such as swaps which cut across traditional product boundaries is a special problem for the highly structured Japanese banks in which the organisation chart reflects seniority rather than expertise. Kunihiko Takai, a senior Bank of Tokyo officer, describes his efforts to create the conditions needed for product innovation:

> **Because our seniority system is not necessarily appropriate for new products, in swap transactions we set up a task force by**

appointing an individual outside the seniority system to take the lead and build a staff around him in London, New York and Tokyo. Most of the staff have their regular job to do as well. As the task force activity becomes well established, it may become an ordinary part of the organisation.

When questioned about new product development, most excellent banks refer to the retail sector and to technology-based products in particular. The interviewer thus usually finds himself talking with the bank's head of data processing services about investment in retail delivery systems and efforts to place interactive terminals with corporate customers. These banks have each developed their own delivery system, usually at considerable expense, in a competitive environment where the incremental profitability of the investment is hazy at best. It is beyond the province of this book to determine how innovative each of the systems is in comparison with competitive products. What is relevant is that each of the banks involved considers it a major innovative product grouping from its own standpoint.

It is in technology-based delivery systems that one finds the closest thing to the product champion which features prominently in *In Search of Excellence*. The environment for such champions is a difficult one. The excellent European banks in particular are risk-averse institutions with a decision-making structure which ensures that even minor investments are closely vetted by all members of the top management team regardless of their competence in EDP. In such consensual organisations it does not take much imagination to picture the barriers before a department head – especially a technician rather than line banker – who insists on spending a vast amount of money with some possibility of failure on the downside and no well-defined incremental revenue stream on the upside.

One such individual is Deutsche Bank's Van Hooven, who has headed its retail business since the early 1960s. As recently as 1959 Deutsche Bank was essentially a wholesale banking institution with virtually no retail business, whereas today retail deposits represent about half of the total. One of the many strong personalities on the bank's *Vorstand*, van Hooven recounts the process:

We saw in 1959 that the current account was the cutting edge and went after wage accounts as the core product. Then we

> realised we had to cross borders, and in 1968 eurocheque was born and has since become the biggest payment system in the world. We needed then to feed the branches with new products. A flexible home loan of up to 100 per cent of valuation was developed; it would be granted in as little as twenty minutes at the branch. We went into credit life insurance, despite our good relationships with the insurance companies [who have strong Directorship ties to the bank] in order to compete for savings.

A similar story is told by S-E-Banken's General Manager for Marketing and EDP, Thomas Glueck. Like Deutsche Bank, S-E-Banken was heavily reliant upon corporate and money market deposits and resolved to build its retail deposit base in the 1960s. A major technology investment resulted in their being the first Swedish bank with on-line, real time EDP. Like Deutsche Bank, they focused on wage accounts despite their short term unprofitability: their target was the overall customer relationship.

Glueck, an electric personality who was brought in to head up a combined marketing/EDP function, analyses the process by which these key decisions were made by senior management:

> There was a lot of debate, lots of brilliance, lots of opposition: the atmosphere was very intense. But there was always someone in the management group who would grasp it, elaborate it and not misunderstand it. We have a lot of unorthodox individuals who have an open mind and are prepared to say 'it sounds important – let's do it, but at half speed'. Was it deliberate fostering of innovation – I don't know.

One of his senior colleagues, Jacob Palmstierna, explains why a positive decision was made:

> In certain areas, you can sit back, but if you lose out in payments systems, you have lost the customer. We have to be aggressive in that area.

Another European EDP product champion is Werner Brupbacher, head of EDP for Swiss Bank Corporation. The first major Swiss bank to introduce real time EDP to all banking areas, it considers itself a leader in European technology. Why did such a conservative institution move so aggressively, particularly when some of its competitors were having major technical problems? Brupbacher admits that:

> It was a unique decision by the Executive Board. They are conservative in a business sense but are wise enough to release creativity and not to be afraid of risk. Maybe it was a question of credibility. The Board was sceptical; we had at least five sessions with them. Our estimates were conservative and we had had a good record. All of our EDP proposals have been accepted.

Other examples in the retail banking sector abound. Toronto Dominion moved relatively quickly into discount brokerage to compete in the affluent customer market. Barclays, one of the largest banks in the world, is proud of having developed the Barclaycard, an industry leader in bank cards. Says General Manager Carden,

> We do not sit on new ideas.

The 'we and they' obstacle faced by staff specialists in selling their ideas is reflected in the comment by HongkongBank's Chairman Michael Sandberg:

> One has one's technical experts, and they tend very often to be backroom boys with high IQs and high academic standing who feed their ideas into the management system. I think one of the strengths of an organisation is to be able to look with enthusiasm at new ideas and not throw up one's hands as probably happened when the wheel was discovered. (*Institutional Investor*, June 1980, p. 40.)

Another product area where some of the excellent banks are active innovators is the capital markets-related sector, which includes the new swap products. Constrained by domestic regulations from direct participation as securities underwriter in their local markets, excellent banks in the US have used product innovation in swaps as the cutting edge of their capital market strategies. All three excellent New York-based banks –

Morgan, Citicorp and Bankers Trust – are market leaders in this highly profitable, rapidly evolving arbitrage product.

How have they done it? Morgan, as mentioned previously, has built in a few years a leadership position in the Euro-bond markets on its capacity for innovation. Administrative head Brackenridge says that

> **The critical factor was co-ordination with the Banking Division, who were the sales force and provided the leadership [of the London unit]. There was support from the top of the bank.**

Walter Gubert, who heads up one of the New York-based units supporting Morgan Guaranty Ltd in London, analyses the environment:

> **Our success in innovation draws on our strong client relationships, our worldwide participation in financing markets, and effective teamwork. Because of our close client relationships, we know their objectives. As a lending participant in worldwide financial markets we have a focus on a wide and ever changing spectrum of opportunities for borrowers and investors. Teamwork among the account officers, our capital markets specialists and very importantly the experts in our client companies pulls it all together so we can match the transaction and market opportunities with a client's objectives. When it works the result is innovation.**

For Bankers Trust's David Beim, the concept of deliberate investment in a R and D-type budget to develop new products makes no sense:

> **The concept of corporate finance as a think tank does not happen in the real world – product development happens through participation as a player in the markets, by bringing people together. We have physically moved capital markets people to the trading floor. Our people in New York, London and Tokyo talk many times each day.**

As could be expected from a bank which cities innovation as part of its corporate credo, Citicorp regards itself as an archetypical innovator. A constant stream of new ideas is generated by this credo, reinforced by a philosophy heard frequently in 399 Park Avenue to the effect that 'no one has a monopoly on good ideas', a deliberate effort to stimulate different – and often competitive – solutions to client problems.

Listen to several Citibankers articulate the philosophy:

Tom Jones, Citibank's chief accounting officer:

> We take the actuarial base and give it a try. There is a freedom to take different approaches.

Rick Roesch, SVP:

> We encourage people to be creative. Citibank is usually the new guy on the block: what do we bring to the party. When a senior officer like Tom Theobold visits his people out in the field, he asks them what new products they have developed.

Byron Knief, SVP and Marketing Director for the North American Banking Group:

> Part of our culture is to be willing to act before we have all the facts. Sticking your neck out forces you to pull it together. We have developed a few truly nationwide segmented delivery systems as a result. We use the 'honey-bee' concept: lots of honey-bees with product responsibility buzzing around with customers and relationship officers. We do not try to define the product but rather ask whether the customer will pay for it.

With the exception of Citicorp and a few others, however, product innovation is neither institutionalised nor dictated from the top. It often seems to be a product of a small group pushing forward an investment proposal in the face of conservative, slow-moving but open-minded top management. As several of the European product champions point out, 'it just happens'. Citicorp's Chairman John Reed agrees:

> We do not have a technical Tsar. We don't try to centrally plan the evolution of our processing base.

One of the issues which must be addressed by those excellent banks broadening their product ranges is their ability to understand and manage their new businesses. Sticking to one's knitting is a virtue cited by *In Search of Excellence* and espoused by virtually all of the excellent banks. For some, it can be argued that they stick too close and risk losing the whole ball of yarn by failing to develop competitive delivery systems or ranges of products.

For cultural and other motives, most excellent banks expanding into securities-related products have done so by internal growth rather than acquisition. The human dimension of this decision will be discussed in Chapter 8. Very few, in fact, of the excellent banks have made significant acquisitions at all in recent years: the most recent mergers, which produced Bayerische Vereinsbank and S-E-Banken, date back to the early 1970s. And friends at the former deem it successful largely because their partner, the Bayerische Staatsbank, accepted Bayerische Vereinsbank's leading role.

One excellent bank which has not hesitated to expand its product base by acquisition is Security Pacific. While relatively small in terms of the commercial banking base, these acquisitions have taken SecPac into a variety of non-bank financial services throughout the world: stockbroking, government securities broking, insurance services and mortgage banking.

Rather than to try to integrate these new activities into the inbred Californian banking system, management has followed a policy of autonomy with central control at a senior level. Cross-selling with the commercial banking business takes place on a negotiated basis. As a friend at SecPac explains:

You have to bid for the bank's business. Dick Flamson [the CEO] says not to rely on the bank for your bottom line.

The same process of negotiation takes place with staff support units – line businesses can go outside if they cannot negotiate a mutually satisfactory deal with the internal unit. A strategic management concept provides each business with profit targets and business objectives from the top.

The bank's 1983 *Annual Report* states the position clearly:

No staff support department has a monopoly on the service it offers. Each must compete with alternative sources in terms of quality and cost.

Vice-Chairman Hartmann describes the negotiation process between his line banking group and other affiliates:

Cross-selling the network is not a new issue. Our insurance subsidiary wanted to get into the business of selling credit life along with our auto loans. We worked out a deal at the top by which the insurance sub hands over a good deal of its revenue to the branch. Its a win–win situation for the customer and all of us. We look at the branch itself as a production centre – how many various products did it sell, rather than what is its profit.

Some of the excellent banks have thus broadened their product lines not just by expanding into established lines but also by developing new electronic delivery systems and capital market products. The European universal banks, while understandably envied by their US and other counterparts, are facing this same issue: how does a large, conservative institution allocate significant human and financial resources to people where there is both a risk of failure as well as considerable uncertainty of financial reward for innovation? Here, arguably, the European universal banks, with their extensive check and balance decision-making structure, may be at a disadvantage. Yet the above examples of articulate and convincing product champions in the EDP or retail functions of some of these banks, coupled with a willingness of their Executive Boards to assume the development risk, shows that such innovation can take place.

The successful product development record of the three New York-based excellent banks in the capital markets sector reflects strong encouragement and support from top management as well as the presence of highly qualified and motivated generalist bankers. Having developed these new capabilities, the challenge for these institutions is now to cross-sell them effectively through relationship and other officers.

Such cross-selling at Morgan and Citibank involves extensive training in the new products, verbal communications and travel. At Morgan, liaison officers are assigned to line banking groups to walk them through the new products. Citibank's Knief points out that:

> **What works we make very visible. Every one of our officers has a computer terminal describing the new product profile and training opportunities, but the best officers do not wait to get trained.**

5 Customers: Segmentation and Proximity

Banking is where the customer is – Nikolaus Senn, Union Bank of Switzerland.

That the customer base is central to a bank's success has long been an implicit foundation stone of bank strategy. One of the more colourful phrases one hears, in a variety of excellent banking accents, is that 'we eat off the customer'. What characterises the excellent banks is their explicit recognition of being market-driven, which leads to the total restructuring of a bank and its priorities around the customer. In the comfortable past, a bank might sit back and dole out scarce resources to its grateful clients. In the competitive 1980s, its survival is a function of differentiating itself in some way from hundreds of rivals with roughly equivalent product lines.

This adaptation to a market-driven role has manifested itself in two broad trends which will be the focus of this chapter. First is the need to move closer to the customer in physical and other respects. Second is the process of segmenting and setting priorities among different groups of clients and prospects. While some excellent banks have been more explicit than others in adapting to market realities, their strategies in general reflect this heightened awareness of customer needs.

Being 'close to the customer' is another theme of *In Search of Excellence*, and the excellent banks have developed a variety of techniques to achieve this goal. Perhaps its most direct manifestation is simple physical contact: the frequency, depth and nature of interface mechanisms.

For Texas Commerce, simple volume of contacts – number of calls made – is one of the limited number of performance indicators used by Chairman Ben Love to evaluate his line colleagues:

> There's an atmosphere of sell, not tell. We quantify it but keep it simple. It sounds terribly unimaginative, but we stick to our knitting: the Texas market, where we have 15 per cent of domestic loans. We audit call reports to make sure we achieve our goal – 115 000 calls this year.

The same emphasis on physical contact is seen at Morgan. One of Morgan's former geographic heads notes that:

> I used to call on forty major clients in New England. Now it's down to three or four. We have a smaller number of major, primary relationships; we have flattened the pyramid by pushing relationships down the structure.

Among the excellent European banks, UBS is a strong advocate of initiating more customer contact. As Chief Executive Senn points out,

> We're fighting to do this. We need more client contact. Banking is where the customer is. We have to do more cross-selling to take advantage of our universal banking product range.

For Citicorp, more simple physical contact is not enough. In recent years, Citibank has undertaken in the US a massive programme of moving its relationship officers, together with support staff, out of New York head office into the field where they will be able to develop stronger personal and functional relationships with corporate clients and prospects. To quote Larry Small, Citicorp's Institutional Bank head in North America,

> We came to the realisation that every major service business in the US had developed a decentralised delivery system to place whatever they were selling next to their clients. By moving Citibank's offices into these communities, they can now live and play with the customers. Our customers have become our neighbours.

EVP Jack Heilshorn explains:

Process is the key, not structure. There's a problem if support for customer relationships is not physically close to the account officer. There is collective goal-setting when we put them together; we create reality through open communication. If bright people get together in the same room, you get different results than is the case in rigid adherence to the hierarchical organisation structure.

Many European banks feel that their matrix structure at the Management Board level is a major factor in improving the management/client interface. To the outsider, giving each Board member line responsibility for a certain geographic region as well as specific functional activities appears to complicate an already top-heavy decision-making structure. To Deutsche Bank's Guth, however, it ensures excellent client contact. As he points out,

It gives you a feel for the 'front line' situation at the main branches and for the client relationship. After a Board meeting, each Board member spreads the gospel by going out into the field himself.

Excellent banks have also made extensive use of the relationship or account officer concept in various forms. From the bank's standpoint, having one officer responsible for interface with a given client facilitates the identification of responsibility as well as ensures that appropriate products are marketed to meet the individual client's perceived needs.

From the client's standpoint, a relationship officer represents a human physical contact with a complex multi-product, multi-unit organisation. John Rudy, EVP for banking services for the leading market research organisation Greenwich Research Associates, describes the corporate customer's needs:

Getting close to the corporate customer requires a role where the banker provides advice. It is the human element, the answer-man, the wise counsellor, 'who do you call when you have a problem?'. You try to build this kind of relationship. How do you do it? It's sold and earned. It's the readiness to go the extra mile. Most institutions haven't developed this capability.

The excellent banks have acknowledged this need but responded with varying levels of explicit commitment. For banks organised on a decentralised basis with a strong commitment to leadership by the local branch manager, giving effective line responsibility to a single relationship officer – especially one located in the head office – constitutes a major restructuring. It also requires a re-jigging of the management information structure to provide global information on a single corporate relationship so that the account officer can both be evaluated himself as well as have useful numbers to work with in developing the relationship. The accounting-based management information system of many banks must be restructured on a matrix basis to meet these needs.

As a result of these constraints, many excellent banks have not identified relationship officers or have made only a limited commitment often on a staff-level basis for major corporate relationships. HongkongBank, Bayerische Vereinsbank and Swiss Bank Corporation thus have not gone over to a relationship management concept on a broad scale.

A friend at Bayerische Vereinsbank says:

We have a relationship concept in theory but not in reality. Whoever is close to the client handles the business. It's sometimes a mess because of the lack of co-ordination. But we're drifting in the right direction.

Other excellent banks use relationship officers on a staff basis to gather information, develop products and provide advice on multinational corporations to the line officers in operating units who actually deal with the clients. Thus Barclays' smaller corporate accounts are still managed in its branches, but the larger ones are handled by a central corporate group. In contrast to most of its Japanese competitors, Sumitomo uses account officers throughout the bank. As a friend there says,

Implicitly, the concept of relationship officers is not so unique in Japan. To do it explicitly as we do *is* unique.

Bank of Tokyo moved early to an account officer concept for thirty to forty major domestic corporate names. Deutsche

Bank's 700 corporate account officers are based in its branches but supported by a strong headquarters staff group. Branch officers are given an array of product and research information which they can use as they wish. In contrast, its headquarters private banking group plays a strong staff and line role *vis-à-vis* the branch officers who serve the bank's five million personal and small corporate customers. Hans-Dieter Spanier, a SVP for retail banking in Frankfurt headquarters, sees the role of his department in supporting the branches and – as an essential part of this – motivating the branch officers who have profit centre responsibility for retail business.

The US and Canadian excellent banks have generally made a much stronger commitment to a relationship officer with significant organisational clout. In the retail sector, Wachovia as mentioned previously introduced the Personal Banker in the 1970s to provide the human link supplementing the interface with automated systems. In the corporate sector, Citibank relationship officers are the fulcrum of its decentralised customer-drive strategy. EVP Heilshorn describes the evolution of the bank's thinking:

> **Back in the 1960s, we were organised by product and geography. We needed committees to focus on the customer. In 1969, we reorganised into decentralised customer groups. We put our talent opposite the customer and organised around his needs to satisfy his service and product requirements.**

One of the weaknesses of the relationship officer concept is the level of experience and seniority of the account officer in comparison with his counterpart in the corporate treasurer's office. In the typical bank's vertical hierarchy, the law of numbers means that relatively junior officers are often given account responsibility while their seniors handle managerial tasks. The US excellent banks are particularly concerned with the resulting mismatch with the corporate treasurer's greater decision-making power and financial expertise.

One solution at Morgan is the 'senior banker', an experienced officer with extensive geographic experience but no particular client or administrative responsibility. Morgan senior bankers around the world play a key role in bringing innovative products to clients at a senior level in support of relatively junior relationship officers. Morgan's Brackenridge describes the process:

> We found the account officers were not getting in to see the client's senior management. Now the junior guy smokes out the deal and brings in the senior banker, who is more transaction-oriented. They are busy as hell.

Bankers Trust is concerned about the same problem. David Beim points out that:

> Investment banking services get sold at higher levels of seniority within client companies. We have very good relationship officers who know their clients very well, but we are pushing relationship management up the organisation and separating it from the lending function.

Another means of responding to client needs is the handling of problems. A traditional policy at Wachovia is that some form of action or acknowledgement must occur the same day as a customer complaint is received. John Medlin explains that:

> Resolving a complaint is a high priority item. It sounds like an overreaction, but it adds to the service atmosphere. We all understand that errors are made; the key is to do something about it.

In addition to Wachovia's Medlin, Toronto Dominion's CEO Thomson also makes a point of seeing complaint letters. Excellent banks have also attempted to move closer to clients through organisational restructuring. In some cases like Bankers Trust, Morgan and Toronto Dominion, the traditional banking pyramid is flattened. In others, a segmented structure is developed to meet the needs of particular client categories.

Toronto Dominion prides itself on what it regards as an extremely flat structure for a bank with a major retail dimension. A branch client is only four levels removed from TD's President; only one of the 900-plus branch managers and a regional division head intervene in the chain of command. One of TD's senior managers comments:

> Such a broad span of control – over a hundred branch managers reporting to a regional manager, and over twenty people reporting to the President – implies lots of mutual trust. We all know each other well and, whatever our personal feelings, are pretty comfortable with each other. In that situation, you do not need to spend a lot of time chasing things up.

Other banks are conscious of the need to reduce the organisational distance between the client and senior decision-makers. One of Deutsche Bank's traditions is the *Herrenabend*, an evening when the *Vorstand* entertains about sixty of its major clients. The US excellent money centre banks such as Morgan and Bankers Trust compare themselves with their much leaner rivals, the Wall Street investment banks, and are taking action to flatten the organisation chart.

Another technique designed to increase responsiveness to customer needs is simply to ask them. Spending on formal and informal market research has ballooned in the past decade as banks have realised that their preconceived image of what the customer wanted did not fit reality. Such research has tended to take two forms: informal contact with one or more clients by bank personnel in what are often known as client panels or focus groups, and formal market research by an outside party. In both cases the objectives are the same. What does the customer think of us? How do we rank among our competition? What can we do better to meet client needs?

The responses have had some fairly cosmic consequences. The arrival of a Greenwich Research report is awaited in many quarters with some trepidation. As mentioned previously, Wachovia set up its Personal Banker concept following a major consumer survey in 1971. At Citibank, Byron Knief describes a continuous client monitoring process:

> We use focus groups where we call in customers to test ideas. There's an annual relationship audit. We have a service audit with the client. Market research is used basically to validate the ideas that come from this process.

At Union Bank of Switzerland, marketing specialist Carl-Gustaf Malmstroem notes that, whereas market research was not used extensively five years ago, the bank has considerably increased the use of client surveys and other market research studies. Deutsche Bank and Toronto Dominion are also heavy users of client panels or focus groups.

At S-E-Banken, a customer survey literally reshaped the bank. International Managing Director Palmstierna relates:

> **Ask your customers – that's the key. McKinsey did – they interviewed thirty of our major corporate clients who said we provided pretty lousy service. This was the basis for a reorganisation to segment our business. We've not only moved the overseas networks and eighty of our large multinational accounts into this function but also operating departments just for them: guarantees, letters of credit, foreign exchange, etc. It works better, there's better quality, we have more fun, and it probably isn't any more expensive to have smaller operating units – the economics of scale are not that important.**

The market research tradition at S-E-Banken remains strong. Every two years an attitude survey of about 700 corporations provides a profile of the bank's image in the market-place. One recent finding has been the bank's association in the public mind with major corporations, and as a result efforts have been concentrated recently on small to medium sized Swedish corporates.

The second major trend in customer relationships is the process of client segmentation and setting of priorities which the above example at S-E-Banken highlights. Most banks have inherited a traditional client profile with a particular focus on one or more client groups. At Morgan and S-E-Banken, it is major corporates. HongkongBank has always been close to entrepreneurial groups, both large and small. Bank of Tokyo, which has a limited domestic base, understandably finds itself focusing on the major Japanese trading companies. Union Bank of Switzerland has traditionally been strong in the sector of small to medium sized Swiss firms.

The pressure of competition and limited resources has obliged such excellent banks to make their distinctions more explicit: to segment these client categories on a more formal basis and to set priorities among existing and potential other segments. Such a process has totally remodelled many of these institutions over the past decade. Deutsche Bank and S-E-

Banken, which at the outset of the 1960s were essentially wholesale banks, have since made a conscious effort to develop their retail funding by an extensive investment in domestic branch networks. Citibank at the end of the 1970s made the same decision by focusing on retail banking in the US and transferring incremental resources from its prior emphasis on international corporate banking. None of these major shifts were painless; Citibank's consumer banking losses in the early 1980s recall S-E-Banken's concern of a decade earlier as the wage earner account went through an unprofitable start-up phase.

Perhaps more painful is the decision to divest oneself of a major activity, and here Bankers Trust is a marvellous case study. Having decided in the late 1970s that the profit potential from wholesale, merchant banking activities was considerably greater than retail banking, it proceeded to put its entire retail operation on the market. Selling off the 'Chevrolet Division', Bankers Trust's EVP Bob Russell recounts,

> was very unsettling. We transferred to other banks over **4000 of a total of 12 500 employees by selling our upstate and consumer banking franchises. It was an on-going process, as the support system had to be shrunk as well. We also found a considerable mismatch between customer demands and our people skills; there was lots of retraining and recruitment to be done.**

A somewhat less drastic customer-driven organisational solution is the restructuring or segmentation of existing businesses and units. The goal of such segmentation has invariably been to provide more responsive service to clients whose needs are recognised to vary widely from segment to segment. At this outset of the process, relationships from the largest corporate to the smallest personal account would have been handled on a geographic basis through the branch or other unit located where the client did his business.

Citibank started the trend with the shift to what are now the Institutional and Individual Banks. Sumitomo set up in the 1970s a corporate banking division following a McKinsey study. Even Morgan Guaranty, for whom major organisational change is a glacial process, merged its international and domestic banking division to form a single Banking Division in

1981 to provide global services to its corporate clients. Deutsche Bank in the late 1970s set up separate corporate and private banking staff groups at Frankfurt headquarters while retaining its decentralised, geographic focus on branch responsibility.

The excellent banks who retain a traditional, geographic-oriented organisational structure in their home market tend to be Continental European institutions like Swiss Bank Corporation who are committed to decentralisation and are unwilling to reduce the perceived importance of the branch manager. The concept of a domestic branch in the role of production unit, as envisaged by Security Pacific and others, is anathema even to European banks like Deutsche and S-E-Banken who have built up major regional and head office customer-segmented staff functions to 'steer, encourage and motivate' their branch office brethren.

For those excellent banks that are committed to a customer-based structure, the current focus is on segmenting the domestic branch network to improve customer service as well as reduce costs. Toronto Dominion, Barclays and Security Pacific are examples of such delivery network reconfiguration.

Roy Hartmann describes the process at Security Pacific by which 41 business banking centres are differentiated from small units:

> **Middle market companies have higher expectations; we need different skills and units to serve them. Branch banking, on the other hand, will focus on the customer and small business with transaction needs up to perhaps $5000, without any specialist skills. A third segment will be specialist businesses like mortgage banking, trust and third party dealer finance.**

At Barclays, 120 units of the bank's domestic network of 2900 have been identified as 'key' branches which sell more sophisticated products. Toronto Dominion is also placing lending and other expertise in major commercially-oriented branches with retail units acting as satellites.

Customer segmentation starting from a zero base demonstrates both the costs of the *de novo* approach as well as those of the multipurpose delivery systems with which traditional networks are encumbered. Citibank's assault on the US market outside its home state of New York is described by Byron Knief:

> Our marketing strategy is proceeding in three major directions. Our 'frontal attack' entails opening new offices across the country; our 'flank attack' involves using our balance sheet as a warehouse facility, and our 'air attack' is our strategy for electronic banking. We are 'wiring' corporate American so that doing business with us from next door or wherever is becoming indistinguishable and commonplace.

A more traditional means of segmentation used particularly by the North American excellent banks is industry/sectoral specialisation. On the legitimate assumption that clients prefer banks who understand their business, specialist groups in shipping, commodities, real estate and energy can be found in the money centre banks like Morgan and Citibank. In Canada, Toronto Dominion is proud of its expertise in cable television. Outside North America, however, the generalist approach is usually adopted, either because of different perceived client needs or the preference for generalist skills.

Part and parcel of a sharper focus on clients and client segments is improved management information which enables the account officer to allocate resources and top management to evaluate performance. Banks like Citibank and Bankers Trust, who have restructured on a segmented basis, have invested considerable sums to develop matrix-based customer profitability information. Others, who invested early in on-line, real time branch automation, have found it relatively inexpensive to add customer profitability information to their present system. The European and Japanese banks who have retained a branch-oriented organisation structure have generally been obliged by rely on manual estimates of customer profitability based on cost and revenue allocations. These allocations are the subject of great debate as they are perceived to threaten the profit allocation traditionally made to the branch network. For the European excellent bank whose culture of a branch-based profit centre system is strong, arguments over such issues as the appropriate internal transfer rate for deposits, the allocation of capital and sharing of fees inevitably carry political as well as accounting implications.

The arguments for such customer information are, however, strong. Even Morgan, whose customer base is relatively narrow and well defined, has found it useful. Bob McKeracher reports that:

> **We've involved in a two-year project to implement a global customer information file based on about 2000 clients grouped in 290 corporate families. It's very revealing in that one had been overestimating the profitability of many of these relationships.**

To summarise, the excellent banks have been driven by their customers to re-evaluate their client priorities, organisational structure, information base and delivery systems. They are much closer to their customers in the sense of physical contact, formal and informal market research and the use of relationship managers who are assuming an increasingly important role in customer interface.

If the ultimate goal is defined as a total commitment to service as articulated in *In Search of Excellence*, or a relationship manager who has in-depth knowledge of both his client and his own bank's capabilities, however, many excellent banks have some distance to travel. To quote Greenwich Research's Rudy:

> **It's a question of training, longevity in the assignment, precept and example. Even the best banks pay a heavy penalty for their gyrations in terms of people. And European bigwigs visiting the US for example spend some time on ceremonial visits to clients but mostly stay within the bank. If younger people can't see successful seniors trying to be close to the client, it's a terrible handicap.**
>
> **Another problem is the conflict between the relationship officer and the product specialist. The account officer is the senior steward; he has to orchestrate the relationship. The client is the loser if the specialist gets the upper hand. And you need a sophisticated MIS to sort it all out. You can't rely on angels.**

6 Organisational Structure

> *We tend to change the bosses, not the relationship managers, and we resist earthshaking changes* – Alfred Brittain III, Bankers Trust Co.

Melding the dimensions of product, client and geography into a single organisational structure has produced a rich mosaic of totally different excellent bank structures. This chapter will examine first the alternative structures used by the excellent banks and then focus on the similarities and trends which emerge from the plethora of different approaches.

Excellent banks typically use an amalgam of geographical, function and product-based organisational dimensions. Functions like personnel and treasury, product groups such as capital markets, and client groups organised geographically or functionally are juxtaposed in the two- or three- dimensional matrix which has characterised banking for the past decade.

What strikes the outside observer first is the wide disparity in terms of three critical variables:

(1) The degree of centralisation of decision-making;
(2) The extent of collective, as opposed to individual, decision-making;
(3) The trade-off between client and geographic predominance.

First, with respect to the extent of centralisation, one finds two types of banks that are committed to decentralisation as a strategy as well as a decision-making structure. As described in Chapter 2, there are those excellent banks like Hongkong-Bank, Swiss Bank Corporation, Barclays and S-E-Banken that have traditionally regarded decentralisation as an organic value which is part of their culture. Then there are banks like Citibank that have espoused it more recently as the most efficient means of running a large, diverse enterprise populated by independent-minded high performers. Citibank's Rick Roesch makes the case for decentralisation:

> **We have a mind set for decentralisation. Given our vision of the financial service business, you can only do it this way. There's a consistent, determined drive to lower more decisions to the business level but to keep control to maintain consistency and keep ideas flowing across businesses.**

In contrast, banks like Morgan, Bayerische Vereinsbank, Bank of Tokyo and Union Bank of Switzerland retain strong centralised decision-making for a variety of reasons. In some cases, the presence of a strong leadership effectively requires physical presence at head office to ensure propagation of the top-down direction. In others, such as Morgan and Bank of Tokyo, a consensual decision-making process promotes the same physical need for proximity.

Whether the bank is decentralised or not in terms of decision-making, the role of a central staff function can vary widely. Centralised banks understandably have strong central personnel, financial planning and other staff departments, but so do many decentralised institutions like Swiss Bank Corporation. The Japanese excellent banks reflect the traditional importance placed in that country on central planning and staff control. As Bank of Tokyo's Takai explains,

> **We're a strange animal with this lifetime employment system in Japan. The key is to get the right people in the right place. One needs the assurance that this principle is strictly observed.**

But among both the excellent Japanese banks there are also doubts, even among senior staff officers, about the strong role played by the staff functions. Says Bank of Tokyo's planning head Fumio Umemoto,

> **There has been a greater role of the staff as we have centralised the decision-making process. But we're now reviewing the Head Office organisation: maybe the staff is getting too important.**

As planning is delegated to business units, the need for a central financial staff is reduced to co-ordinating the plans of the units. The desirability of a central personnel function is, however, more widely accepted to ensure effective career path planning and the meeting of training and recruitment needs. Toronto Dominion's Urban Joseph makes the case:

> **We've centralised credit, personnel and little else. We decentralised the areas that affect the customer. Our corporate resource programme, made up of high potential people identified as 'corporate staff', represents about 600 to 700 officers and trainees, and their career management and compensation is handled centrally.**

Several of the decentralised banks use relatively autonomous units competing with each other to take full advantage of their people skills. In other organisations, rationalisation would eliminate what might appear to be a duplication or resources. Citibank encourages competition among its business units; as Jack Heilshorn says,

> **Redundancy is the price we pay for decentralisation and sustaining an entrepreneurial environment for the best and the brightest people.**

Others agree. Swiss Bank Corporation's three major Swiss branches compete in the international money and foreign exchange markets and have their own international correspondent functions, while Deutsche Bank's main domestic branches each have their independent securities market activities.

The second dimension of organisational structure is the balance between individual and collective decision-making. At the former extreme are Citibank and HongkongBank who rely on individual decision-makers for credit as well as non-credit decisions. In sharp contrast are European banks like Swiss Bank Corporation and Deutsche Bank whose commitment not just to democracy, but also to unanimity is part of their culture.

In between are those with a strong tradition of consensus or open informal communications: Morgan, Toronto Dominion and Bank of Tokyo. Even in banks like Bayerische Vereinsbank and Union Bank of Switzerland with strong top-down leadership, there is good feedback and communications within the senior management team. At Texas Commerce, for example, a committee system is used to discuss and communicate on issues, whereas at the German and Swiss banks the management board structure ensures that communication takes place regardless of how the ultimate decision is made.

The apparent satisfaction of the excellent banks with such a variety of decision-making systems confirms that there is no magic or ideal point in the individual–collective spectrum. For those at the collective end, however, the burdens imposed by volume and diversity of work are considerable. To quote Deutsche Bank's Dr Guth:

> **Having a full matrix of responsibilities – both functional and geographic – imposes a great burden on board members. Frequently they have an overload of work, and there is an argument for reappraising the situation. But thus far we have not found a better solution.**

Members of the Management Board of the excellent German and Swiss banks do indeed work extremely hard to follow developments in their own areas of responsibility, review credits and sit as Board members reviewing the work of other areas. In addition, one can argue that it is unrealistic to expect that one individual can effectively handle such a wide range of staff and line responsibilities. One indication of a possible trend away from a totally collective decision-making process can be found in the recent decision by the Bank of Tokyo to join other collectively-managed banks in setting up standing board committees on credit, asset/liability management and other functions so as to improve the speed of the decision-making process.

The third dimension of organisational diversity is the trade-off between client and geographic orientation. Banking has traditionally grown up with responsibility attached to geographic location, and banks like HongkongBank, Swiss Bank Corporation and S-E-Banken have retained this original orientation. Even in the most client-oriented structure – Citibank, Bankers Trust, and Deutsche Bank – client responsibilities are still assigned largely on a geographic basis. The trade-off between client and geography thus remain dynamic and unresolved.

Organisational Structure

What has departed, however, is the matrix concept by which a given line manager would report to two bosses. In this sense, matrix management among some of the US excellent banks has come and gone. It can still be found in staff functions such as personnel and financial control, but as a device for line management it was found overly complex and demotivating. The current situation at Citibank is described by Tom Jones:

> **It's rare to have a dual reporting relationship with two solid lines. In staff areas such as financial controllers of our 200 businesses, there's a carrot and stick approach: the current performance review of such a controller is handled by the line manager of the business, but the senior staff officer for financial control determines his promotion prospects.**

Attitudes towards organisational change also tend to vary widely among the excellent banks. While there is general agreement that relatively minor changes should be made periodically, there is great resistance among most of the banks to the type of perpetual market-driven restructuring cited in *In Search of Excellence*.

The Japanese banks, with their tradition of seniority-related structure, clearly find major restructuring difficult, and the recent consolidation of head office functions was a major event for the Bank of Tokyo. In the excellent Swiss and German banks, portfolios change around within the Management Board, but the basic structures have remained fairly constant in recent years.

At the other extreme are some of the US and other banks which do indeed espouse the concept of continual adaptation to the demands of the market-place. Wachovia's CEO Medlin explains:

> **Our organisation structure may change every year in one way or another. It's built around people as well as being market-driven. It thus has to be an evolving thing.**

Dr Guth of Deutsche Bank agrees:

> **There's no perfect organisation. You only know if it's the wrong one. We constantly discuss possible improvements. From time to**

time – not too frequently – we feel a need for organisational changes, particularly in areas with new developments such as investment banking.

Citibank managers understandably echo this view. Some, however, are prepared to acknowledge that it can be overdone. As one Citibank excutive admits:

> Sometimes we have violent swings of direction *vis-à-vis* customers. We move people around and change our business philosophy too often. In some countries, we've had four or five different iterations of strategy.

On balance, most excellent banks agree that what is important is not change in itself but what is changed and how it is done. The primacy of the stable relationship officer is one agreed goal. Bankers Trust's CEO Brittain expresses a common view:

> It scares me to have as a principle of management the jarring of the organisation to keep people in tune with the market. But the organisation is a living thing: you can't lock it up. Continuity in certain markets is worth a lot. We tend to change the bosses, not the relationship managers, and we resist earthshaking changes.

The view is echoed by Morgan's EVP of banking, Peter Smith,

> We did not change, as result of the 1981 reorganisation, one person who was in contact with a customer. (*Euromoney*, May 1982.)

Another common theme among excellent banks is the preparation for organisation change. The guidelines are communication and consensus. Toronto Dominion's Richard Thomson notes that:

> We do not have organisational revolutions; it all evolves slowly so as not to disrupt the customer and our own people. In corporate banking, we took fourteen years to introduce the account officer concept.

Morgan management agrees. As Bruce Brackenridge explains:

We change by decades. It's so evolutionary people do not notice. Setting up a single Banking Division was a non-event; we had been talking about it for a long time.

A common organisational trait of the excellent banks is the presence of a variety of devices to ensure effective communications and the resolution of conflicts. In banks with a strong consensual tradition such as Swiss Bank Corporation and Morgan, elimination of conflict through informed communication is a very natural process.

In highly decentralised banks like Citibank, the level of internal conflict is naturally stimulated by the presence of a team of over-achievers and, as Citibank's Larry Glenn explains,

The assumption is that no one has all the answers. Sometimes there's too much internal conflict. We let it rip but do try to make sure that people communicate. It's a necessary product of our goals and values.

Adds Jack Heilshorn:

The key question is whether the internal competition is destructive in terms of the customer; our culture says that customer service is the key. Turf issues are inevitable.

In other banks with a tradition of strong personalities either at the top or elsewhere in the organisation, conflict resolution can take several forms. As pointed out in Chapter 2, most conflicts are resolved by intensive discussion at the staff level at Deutsche Bank. Others go to the *Vorstand* with the implicit assumption that the traditional unanimous verdict will be accompanied by a closing of ranks and support for the decision. The process in the excellent Continental European banks takes time, but the resulting agreement is accepted as being worth the delay. Among the Japanese banks, the traditional bottom-up decision-making process ensures a similar cohesion.

The informal decision-making process is a strong one at banks like Texas Commerce and Security Pacific with strong leadership from a chief executive whose views are well known throughout the organisation. A Texas Commerce senior staff officer points out that:

> On the one hand, there is great concern that responsibility be identified and great pains taken with job descriptions. On the other hand, in practice, the winners in this bank do not let the organisation get in their way. The losers tend to take organisational responsibility seriously.

Comments another senior line officer at Texas Commerce:

> The organisation chart shows all 69 subsidiary bank managers reporting to Ben Love. In practice, just about everyone in the bank does.

The same theme is heard at Security Pacific. CEO Richard Flamson conducts 'skip sessions' named for organisation levels he skips in his communications with lower levels of management.

In other banks, the informal mechanisms are sufficiently strong that there is no felt need for an organisation chart to be widely disseminated inside and outside the organisation. Deutsche Bank, Citibank and HongkongBank fall into this category. A common phrase heard in such organisations is that 'we all know what's expected of us'.

In summary, the excellent banks have each developed a pattern of organisational behaviour which reflects their particular culture and leadership style. There is a profusion of responses in terms of the trade-offs between individual and collective, centralised and decentralised, client and geographic-based.

Yet there are several common themes. The first is strong communications, both upward and downward depending on the culture of the particular bank. In banks like Wachovia, Citibank and Deutsche Bank one continually hears the phrase 'freedom of speech' used to confirm that disagreeing openly with one's boss or even chief executive is not a mortal sin.

As a result, decisions are effectively made and conflicts resolved after a level of internal debate which varies according to the organisation's particular culture. And the decisions tend to stick, either because of the strength of the consensus reached or the forcefulness of the leader who expresses them.

A corollary of the high level of communication is a strong informal process which transcends the formal organisation structure. Once again, the strength of the informal process may reflect either a natural, cultural instinct for consultation or be the product of a strong leadership whose views are known and respected up and down the organisation.

There are no clear trends that characterise the excellent bank structures. Most bankers would agree with Dr Guth that it is not a question of finding an ideal structure but of making one work through an effective communication and decision-making process. One can also, however, detect a desire for simplification of structure on the part of the European banks who have traditionally lived with a totally collective process. Conceivably some of these banks will move towards greater specialisation of function at the Management Board level in the future.

7 Leadership: The Chief Executive's Role

I'm literally running for office every day to fight for their hearts, minds and approval – John Medlin, Wachovia.

At the top of each excellent bank organisation is a chief executive whose role is the subject of this chapter. The understandable temptation to use the chief executive as a microscope to discover the secret of excellence is immediately thwarted by yet another rich profusion – this time of leadership styles. These range from the totally shared leadership role at Swiss Bank Corporation and Deutsche Bank to the charismatic, top-down leadership at Texas Commerce and UBS. What patterns of leadership are therefore found among the excellent banks? And are there any common themes or patterns which can help the outsider to relate leadership to excellence?

First, a caveat. Not all of the sixteen chief executives were available for an interview. On the other hand, the comments made in these instances by their senior colleagues permit the observer to fill in quite a few pieces of the puzzle.

When asked about their role, the chief executives provide an almost bewildering array of responses which reflects their personal style, their bank's culture and their perception of the current challenges faced.

To start first at the German and Swiss banks which pride themselves on a presumed *lack* of leadership: Deutsche Bank and Swiss Bank Corporation. At the latter, the Chairman is a member of a Board of Directors which, in traditional Swiss Federalist tradition, rotates its chairmanship on an annual basis. As one of his senior staffers explains:

His job is to make Executive Committee meetings run more efficiently. He sets the agenda priorities and guides discussion.

There's not a big external role. Switzerland as a country has lots of experience in compromise. There's an intuitive feeling of not stepping on toes.

The Chairman attends meetings of the Executive Committee of seven general managers of equal status which effectively runs the bank. While the current Chairman Franz Galliker acknowledges that the freedom to disagree at Executive Committee level is 'sometimes too much', there is general agreement among members that, as one put it:

> The bigger we become, the more appropriate our decentralised, Federalist style is.

The same philosohy is reflected at Deutsche Bank whose twelve *Vorstand* members are considered equal in every respect, from salary to their ability to veto a decision. A reflection of this equality is the current practice of splitting the speaker, or *Sprecher* of the Board, role into two co-speakers. Dr Guth, one of the two speakers, analyses his function in this environment:

> Like all Board members, I provide motivation to subordinates and bring in business through my contacts. As co-speaker, I try to devote sufficient time to strategy and present the image of the bank to the world. My weekly task in alternation with Dr Christians is to moderate *Vorstand* meetings. It can sometimes be very strenuous, given all the strong temperaments, but I try to steer the group. This is most likely the greatest responsibility for Dr Christians and myself.

In addition to these multiple burdens, Dr Guth carries his share of the traditional Deutsche Bank functional and geographic line responsibilities. There has been a shift of emphasis in the Deutsche Bank leadership role. As Dr Guth explains:

> When I joined the *Vorstand*, more than half of its time was spent on individual transactions. Each member is still eager to bring deals to the table, but more time is spent now on strategy and co-ordination. Our Board meetings devote four-fifths of their time to strategy: looking ahead, looking at opportunities; and

one-fifth to transactions. **Our style has changed with our size.**

In other excellent banks, this role of the chief executive as discussion leader or committee chairman becomes the more forceful one of arbiter or resolver of conflicts. In S-E-Banken an Executive Management Board of five Managing Directors has the executive function. As Chairman Olsson points out, conflict resolution is one of his key roles:

> There's a productive tension. We're frank with each other and always moving, although not always in the same direction. If one gets out of line, the others can be expected to put him back on track. My role is to follow local decisions, monitor performance and raise issues. If there's a disagreement over credit risk, I might have the final say on behalf of the Board of Directors. But more important, the group feels the pressure to search for a consensus, and it has actually never happened that we have not been able to reach an agreement. I try to keep informed by regular reporting and by attending the regional Board meetings. It's management by exception.

At Wachovia, the resolution of conflicts is only one of John Medlin's many roles. He describes the hats he wears:

> I have four bosses – the shareholders, the customers, the employees and the public, and there's a continual communication with all four. I'm literally running for office every day to fight for their hearts, minds and approval. Within the bank, there's an on-going process of feeding people with our philosophy, which starts when they're hired and I tell them what to expect from the organisation. There is inherent tension and conflicts of interest in banking among the three critical functions – business development, credit administration and funding management – and I have to arbitrate among the people responsible for these functions. I'm also the overall planner; each group has its own plan and I bring it together.

CEO Medlin's role probably best approximates the conventional perception of the leader as manager. This is confirmed by the frequency with which various outside organisations have bestowed on him the accolade of being one of the top US bank chief executives.

Another role played by many of the excellent banks' chief executives is that of the commanding general. The military analogy is appropriate in that guidelines are simple and straightforward, responsibilities are clear and hierarchical, and performance is consistently rewarded or punished. Bayerische Vereinsbank, Union Bank of Switzerland and Texas Commerce have leaders which reflect this top-down role. UBS' Dr Senn articulates his leadership position:

> **My job is to co-ordinate a huge, growing bank. We've formed a real team of top people; I ensure that they do not go off in different directions. I'm the reserve division which intervenes when necessary, including in our political and economic environment. The Executive Board meets weekly; we discuss with the Chairman and the Vice-chairmen, and the following Monday the whole top management receives the report.**

Strong, simple and clear guidelines with a focus on performance is also the leadership theme at Texas Commerce. Chairman Ben Love explains his management philosophy:

> **I believe in simplicity and the need to quantify. We have evolved a system of five simple, quantified objectives. The best informed organisation will make the best decisions. We have a seventeen-page monthly analysis of all key ratios for each unit. I do not have to say anything: the numbers are accepted as fair. I also have to know the market-place, so I see clients and spend some time every year with each of our banks.**

CEO Love's colleagues speak of his strong leadership, his appetite for work and the force of his personality. Little imagination is required to picture the pressure on the unfortunate manager who comes bottom of his peer group in the monthly *Blue Book* without a good explanation. Of all the excellent banks, the association between bank and leadership is perhaps the closest at Texas Commerce, with the understandable concern expressed by both insiders and outsiders as to the structure and future of the bank following Ben Love's eventual retirement.

Several chief executives perceive their principal role as the vehicle by which the bank's culture and strategic direction are transmitted throughout an often vast and growing organisation. Such a role requires visibility and constant communications as well as the need to resolve conflicts which threaten the culture and direction.

Such traits are present in most of the excellent banks, but they are well expressed by Morgan's Preston:

> **There's a terrific emphasis on communications; we make sure the strategic direction is understood by everybody. A lot of thought goes into career path planning. We also emphasise teamwork by trying to single out transactions involving a variety of different offices and disciplines. I repeat the admonition that profit centres are a management control device; anybody caught worrying about profit centres rather than the overall benefit of the bank is guilty of bad judgement.**

Much the same philosophy is articulated by Bankers Trust's Brittain:

> **My role as CEO is to complete the acceptance of Bankers Trust as an excellent merchant bank with its culture firmly in place. The process started in 1978 and it will probably take another three years [to 1987] to achieve it. I move quickly to explain to our people what the rules are. We've had to drop a few people every year either to improve productivity or emphasise common purpose. I use lots of stories of common purpose, which is our culture.**

Another role often played by chief executives is that of senior lending officer or deal maker. While most US excellent bank chief executives are rarely involved in credit decisions on a systematic basis, the hierarchical credit structure of many others requires the chief executive to provide his approval of the larger exposures. Thus at Bayerische Vereinsbank, S-E-Banken, Union Bank of Switzerland, Toronto Dominion and HongkongBank the chief executive plays a more or less active role as the ultimate credit decision-maker. As pointed out earlier by Dr Guth of Deutsche Bank, this role is increasingly being delegated to other senior colleagues, but the relationship between banking and credit granting is a living one even at the top of most excellent European banks.

At HongkongBank, the chief executive in addition plays the role of senior deal maker in the context of the bank's strategic expansion programme. The bank having decided to expand geographically by major acquisitions, Chairman Michael Sandberg has played a central role personally in the negotiation of the deals.

At Toronto Dominion, CEO Richard Thomson combines many of the leadership roles discussed above. He summarises them as follows:

> First, I have to be aware of what's going on in the market and in the bank. It helps to have been around a long time; solving most problems has to be done by investing in the long term. Secondly, I have to be accessible to all levels of management and to jump levels, if necessary. I move around a lot and talk with people. We also have a shared decision-making structure in the credit process, and I get involved.

What common threads can be drawn from this *pot-pourri* of different styles, goals and cultures? A lot more, in effect, than from a study of organisational structure.

First of all, leadership reflects a bank's cultural values. At Morgan, Wachovia, Toronto Dominion, Bankers Trust and Swiss Bank Corporation, it is clear that one of the leaders' principal roles is to reinforce these values. In most cases, the leaders have grown up with values, and the two are almost indistinguishable. An open, communicative culture understandably requires the leader to be seen and heard – if possible – in the far corners of the organisation. For a bank like Bankers Trust in the midst of cultural change, such a leadership role is central to the success of its new strategy.

By the same token, a change in leadership may threaten values unless the successor provides essentially the same signals. The succession to strong leaders like Ben Love will thus be of interest for more than the usual reasons associated with the transfer of power.

One hears the phrase 'partnership' expressed in many excellent banks to describe a culture reflecting open and strong communication. A senior HongkongBank staff officer describes his bank as a 'partnership, not a corporation; it's like Morgan'. The latter's management probably would not object to this analogy, which recalls its own founding fathers. And Bankers Trust is moving in the same direction as it flattens its structure and emulates its Wall Street competitors.

Secondly, leadership is a matter of what leaders do rather than what they say. Precept and example abound in the excellent banks. Subordinates of these leaders confirm this on countless occasions:

> **Ben Love is always ahead of the rest of us.**
> **Lew Preston does not like surprises.**
> **Dr Senn is not God, but he's a leader who puts the bank first, and few disagree.**
> **No one works harder than John Medlin.**
> **At Deutsche Bank we see the Management Board working very hard – it sets an example.**

Jacob Palmstierna of S-E-Banken sums up his bank's 'do, not say' philosophy:

> **Everybody talks about profits, but there's a difference between what is preached and what is done. Employees are influenced by what management does, not what it says. If I do not control costs, people won't believe me.**

And one thing the excellent CEOs do is work hard. Carrying the burden of executive responsibility in a collectively managed German or Swiss bank leads to long hours. Anyone who questions their commitment to work might well drop into the Deutsche Bank's *Vorstand* office area around 8 p.m. of an evening to witness the level of activity. One can argue that there are simpler ways to run a bank, but it is not part of the culture.

A third trait of the excellent bank's leadership is strong and consistent guidance over an extended perid of time. A CEO may have a light hand or a heavy one on the throttle, but the train has been going in the same direction for years, if not decades. A phrase spoken by a senior Bank of Tokyo officer referring to CEO Watanabe – 'You know what is expected of you' – is heard with a variety of accents and names of CEOs throughout the excellent banks. A Barclays General Manager attributes its managerial strength to the tradition of a full-time executive chairman – unique among British clearing banks. A drastic change of direction such as Bankers Trust's is rare.

The Continental banks are the most eloquent about consistency. Franz Lütolf, a Swiss Bank Corporation Executive Board member, declares that:

> We do not switch each time the wind blows from another direction.

Echoes a senior Toronto Dominion lending officer:

> We do not fall in and out of love with industries.

Arguably one of the exceptions to this thesis is Citibank, whose changes of business strategy have been relatively frequent. And one Citibank SVP, when asked about any possible weaknesses of that formidable institution, agrees:

> We try too hard to make things happen. The elephant has a certain gestation period. We have not got enough patience.

For Bankers Trust, CEO Brittain's turnaround will have taken nine years to implement. It is no wonder that excellent CEOs talk of strategy determination being only 10 per cent, with actual execution representing 90 per cent, of the task at hand.

Another theme of excellent leadership is the common need to exercise authority – whether chairing a committee at Swiss Bank Corporation, approving a major loan at S-E-Banken or sorting out a profit centre squabble at Morgan. Even in the most collectively managed banks, problems drift to the top. Such decisions frequently involve a judgement call – on interest rates, credit, people or compensation. And there is no particular reason why the busy CEO's judgement should be clearly superior to anyone else's.

The strong culture of the excellent banks should provide guidelines and a support mechanism which are perhaps not present in an institution without such a good road map. There is inevitably a certain amount of what Curt Olsson calls 'productive tension' at the top of an excellent bank – in some obviously more than others. Yet the successful CEOs seem to have relied on consistency of direction as well as strong culture to facilitate their task. Office politics probably exist everywhere, but consistent leadership, a strong value system and clear direction should considerably limit its scope.

A final common theme of excellent leadership is visibility. 'Management by walking around' exists in excellent banks as well as excellent companies. It can take many forms other than the traditional image of a Richard Thomson or John Medlin dropping in on people around the bank. It can be the constant interface in the dialogue between a European or Japanese Management Board on credit and other issues. As an excellent Swiss bank's senior credit officer explains,

> **The Board knows the 'handwriting' of all the credit officers through regular credit presentations.**

Or it can be the habit of a Richard Flamson or Ben Love of telephoning several levels down in the organisation to check something out. Things can be tougher in a far-flung branch network; Toronto Dominion's President Robin Korthals covers about seventy of TD's 1000 branches in a year, but the intent is acknowledged.

8 Human Resources: The Care and Feeding of Excellence

What distinguishes this bank starts at the recruitment process – Lewis Preston, Morgan.

We need more broadly based managers – maybe not even with bank training – Kurt Steuber, Swiss Bank Corporation.

Banks are quick to emphasise the importance of people as a key success factor. Phrases like 'we're no better than our people' and 'we're a people business' flow quickly from their lips and public documents. Faced with the obvious wide differential in banking performance, the outsider is hard pressed to determine whether such a phrase is a serious commitment or simply a throwaway line of the type appended as an afterthought to the chairman's statement in Annual Reports.

The excellent banks are no different from others in affirming the importance of their human resources. As indicated in Chapter 2, most excellent banks honestly *do* regard their people as their competitive strength and of significant cultural value. The obvious question is what they do to build this strength. What kind of people do the excellent banks recruit? How are they trained? On what basis are they evaluated and prepared for greater responsibility? And how is performance rewarded – or punished?

The goals of this chapter are:

(1) To describe how excellent banks deal with these issues;
(2) To identify some common trends;
(3) To discuss issues arising from these trends which affect most of the excellent banks.

8.1 SELECTION

Excellent banks to an overwhelming extent grow their own people. Their strong cultures call for entry at the completion of formal education, whether it be secondary school or a graduate business school. The training and job rotation programmes are designed to provide both the necessary functional and managerial experience. 'Outsiders' are recruited as a last resort only to fill specialist requirements which can only be supplied internally with great difficulty: foreign nationals to run an overseas unit, systems specialists, and individuals with expertise in swaps or other new products.

Exceptions to this general rule are the excellent banks going through a major strategic and cultural change. Bankers Trust has thus recruited heavily in the capital markets sector, while Security Pacific has brought in skills in non-bank financial services through both recruitment and acquisition.

Aware that such in-breeding offers disadvantages as well, the excellent banks clearly believe that the advantage of shared values with a single employer more than offsets the possibilities of parochialism and rigidity in the face of change. All of the excellent banks speak of the need for trust, open communications and self-confidence which stem from a lifetime of working together for a firm which promotes internally and provides a 'family feeling'. Morgan's CEO Preston speaks for the other excellent banks in pointing out that:

> **What distinguishes this bank starts at the recruitment process with the involvement of senior management.**

A First Vice-President in Deutsche Bank's Personnel Department, Sigurd Schmidt, articulates the philosophy:

> **We breed our own people from the beginning. Knowing someone from the early years, following him for decades, inviting him to change course from time to time creates a broad-minded, experienced individual who can adapt to the market.**

The unsurprising corollary of such cultural inbreeding is a tendency to reject those who do not espouse these values or who are brought in from the outside in mid-career with different values. One hears the following comments from senior officers:

> The people who leave are outsiders – they could not live with our controls – Texas Commerce.

> You're free not to accept the culture, but it ensures that the leading people are committed; if you do not like it, you can leave it – Bayerische Vereinsbank.

> If you don't like to cooperate, we understand it, and you can leave – Bankers Trust.

> The internal competition is terrifying; people from the outside don't have a chance – Citibank.

While acknowledging a limited need for outsiders with specialist skills, the excellent banks have not been particularly successful in integrating them. HongkongBank's Deputy Chairman Purves comments:

> We prefer to grow our own people but we need some of them from outside with new ideas. I'd guess, however, that about half of them haven't worked out.

Repeats UBS' Dr Senn:

> We sometimes need technical people with special skills.

Given the strong internal cultures and the presumption that only marginal needs should be met by outside hiring, it does not take much imagination to understand why so many of the 'outsiders' have returned once again to the outside world.

What qualities do the excellent banks look for in their recruiting efforts? The prototype is the hard working, committed team player with strong interpersonal skills. A strong culture based on open communication and commitment to bottom line performance demands these qualities. Among the German banks, there is a special emphasis on being able to handle stress. As a Bayerische Vereinsbank manager points out:

[CEO] Hackl likes courageous people who can say no to him. We're looking for real individuals, even if they're difficult to handle. Someone with lots of patience, used to working his way up, and able to cooperate. In a word, an experienced soldier who's difficult to kill.

For a lifetime employer like the Bank of Tokyo, selection is critical. As Bank of Tokyo's Takai points out,

> The key to lifetime employment is getting the right people in the right place with a seniority system. We hire the best people – with creativity, flexibility and farsightedness.

At Citibank and Texas Commerce, the emphasis is on high performers. CEO Ben Love focuses on

> people who are in the top 10 per cent of their class and who have formed the habit of achievement. Bright people are more disciplined and accustomed to achievement.

Citibank also looks for the top performers. Walter Wriston's willingness to 'bet on brains' is reflected in human resources' head Rick Roesch's emphasis on 'those who strive for excellence, team work, creativity, hard work and perceptiveness'. Citibanker Byron Knief describes the recruitment policy as one of

> Hiring as many overachievers as possible with an inordinate amount of energy; then raise them very high.

The frequent reference to 'team player' has different meanings for different institutions. For some, it means an individual prepared to take orders as a good soldier. In others, it relates to contributing as part of a team and subordinating one's own personal wishes to those of the institution. Such a delicate mix is articulated by Citibank's Rick Braddock:

> We win based on teamwork, but we manage in a very aggressive, competitive environment. It's very stimulating and not for the faint of heart.

By the same token, the excellent banks are quite specific as to who they do *not* want to recruit. One hears the phrases 'prima donna' (Swiss Bank Corporation and Wachovia); lone wolf or *Einzelganger* (Deutsche Bank); 'grandstanders' (Morgan); and 'people who want to get rich quickly' (Toronto Dominion).

In a word, even the most aggressive, stressful and profit-oriented excellent bank wants individuals prepared to co-operate and compromise if this is determined to be in the institution's interest.

The excellent banks differ widely in the level of education of the candidate. At one extreme are the US banks, Hongkong-Bank and Bank of Tokyo who now recruit almost exclusively college or business school graduates on the assumption that individuals with a strong record of academic performance are most likely to develop superior technical and managerial skills. At the Bank of Tokyo, for example, the bank traditionally recruits every year around 100 of the top graduates of Tokyo and other major Japanese universities. Only selected government jobs may be considered to have more prestige. Bank of Tokyo is also unique in populating all key areas of the bank with university graduates. The entire Head Office dealing team, for example, is composed of such individuals.

At the other extreme are the Swiss and German banks who have historically hired primarily non-college graduates for an apprenticeship programme designed to select out superior management candidates regardless of educational background. At some of these banks one senses an implicit prejudice against college or business school graduates. Deutsche Bank's Schmidt expresses a common view:

We need élites but not with excessive self-awareness and advancement expectations right from the beginning. University graduates go through the same apprenticeship training but with some modifications.

Echoes a friend at Swiss Bank Corporation:

We hire the best as long as they behave like average people.

The winds of change, however, are blowing through the recruitment process. Swiss Bank Corporation is increasing the proportion of university graduates hired. In the 1970s, HongkongBank switched from a policy of recruiting British public school (high school equivalent) graduates to one of hiring university graduates for its international cadre. Texas Commerce goes for the top 10 per cent of a graduating class for its achievers. Toronto Dominion now hires 20 per cent of its intake at the MBA level. Morgan is increasing its efforts to recruit a greater proportion of the top 20 per cent of MBAs. Security Pacific is a relatively recent convert to hiring MBAs.

High achievers or not, new recruits are transformed into team players whose efforts are focused on corporate rather than personal goals. Wachovia's John Medlin expresses a common view:

> **We want long distance runners, not sprinters. We don't get the fast track people. Our training process makes extraordinary performers out of ordinary people.**

Several excellent banks place a premium on entrepreneurial skills. Citibank (naturally), HongkongBank, S-E-Banken and Security Pacific all articulate the need for self-starting idea-generators. Toronto Dominion's President Korthals explains why:

> **It's pretty hard to convince the branch manager out in the boondocks that we're so excellent. What matters to him is that the competitors can advertise and he can't. That's his universe. The solution is to get him to think as a proprietor. I spend most of my time trying to allow them to grow in the job.**

8.2 TRAINING

Growing one's own talent, coupled in most cases with an implicit commitment to provide career-long employment, places a very special burden on the training function. The burden is particularly heavy for those whose intake is largely composed of teenagers without the base of a liberal or professional education.

Training is thus a central feature of the excellent bank's strategy. A Morgan Vice-President sums it up by saying:

> **Our training programme is the crucible for our culture. The trainees live and work together for six to nine months in a very intense way. They work and play hard together. They know they can count on each other in the future.**

For German and Swiss banks who rely heavily on high school-level recruits, the apprenticeship-based training provides more than technical skills. Waldemar Jacob of Union Bank of Switzerland's personnel function describes their philosophy:

> **Our competitive strength is the number of young people who have been guided and formed as they grow up as apprentices at our Wolfsberg training school. They get to know the philosophy of the bank and grow with it. We enlarge their horizon at every level – not just technical banking expertise. Their background isn't important; we've had MBAs who have failed. There's no streaming at all, although university graduates learn quickly and usually take only two rather than five years.**

A similar training philosophy prevails at Deutsche Bank. Sigurd Schmidt describes it:

> **We take 2000 out of 55 000 applicants a year mainly at the *Abitur* [high school] level. They'll be given a universal training with no early specialisation; perhaps by their late 30s or early 40s they'll go into a final job. Our training system fulfils a communications role: 50 per cent of the outcome is communication. There's a special family atmosphere at our training centre at Kronberg; the *Vorstand* goes there once a week to talk to the trainees, and middle management spends perhaps a week there each year.**

This involvement by top management in the training process is vital for many excellent banks. Morgan's Preston, S-E-

Banken's Olsson and Wachovia's Medlin also make it a point to establish two-way communications with trainees at an early stage.

The 'family feeling' propagated at a training centre is central to the communications process. Loyalties and relationships of trust established even during a brief seminar together become the basis for joint problem solving over the telephone in future years. One of the distinctive characteristics of HongkongBank is its international cadre of about 500 who train together and are posted in three-year development assignments around the globe. Decision-making is facilitated when the decision makers have a hands-on knowledge of both the unit and the people involved.

The role of training as a communications vehicle is confirmed at Union Bank of Switzerland, which regards its management school at Wolfsberg in Switzerland as the key to its human resource strategy. Returning to Wolfsberg as a middle manager to participate in a one week seminar is part of the communications as well as training process, as UBS's Jacob reports:

> We have too much paper in the bank, but we'd have a lot more if we did not have Wolfsberg.

The importance of a common training vehicle is perhaps best demonstrated by those who have hitherto done without it. S-E-Banken is such a case. Its recruitment is largely at the high school level, and its decentralised philosophy does not have room for a central personnel or training function. One of Chairman Olsson's top priorities has been to establish a management school to broaden the outlook of its managerial staff. Set up in late 1984 and named the Wallenberg Institute after one of S-E-Banken's founding fathers, it has raised a variety of issues. Annika Sandstroem, who was brought in from outside the bank to head it up, describes the process:

> There had been no real management training – it was all focused on technical banking issues. We need more adaptability in the bank: here people have been stuck since an early age in an organisation where very little has happened whereas outside there's been a total restructuring of Swedish industry. Now

S-E-Banken has to jump, and the question is whether we have the right people for this jump.

There are no peer models for the Wallenberg Institute. We want to strengthen the political and social competence of our managers, to have them see the bank from the outside, to make them all-rounders. One of the results has been the opening up of debate on questions like 'why do we do it this way' since I try to tie all the discussions back to the bank in a practical sense. Most people are really energised; things are starting to happen.

One of the acknowledged leaders in bank training is Citibank. With an annual global training expenditure in excess of $10 million on credit training alone and five regional training centres around the world, Citibank's managerial culture is fostered by a continual emphasis on training at all career stages. Rick Roesch explains Citibank's approach:

The underlying thought is that our people must stay with the state of the art. We instil marketing concepts through training. As you build new technology, you have to reconfigure people with a longer training programme. At the top of the training pyramid are programmes keyed to values, such as managing people. This has to be uniform: leadership, goal setting, understanding needs, and so forth. Below this are technology-based courses for certain businesses. Underneath are marketing courses geared for certain geographic markets. At the base level, individual businesses do what is appropriate for themselves. We do not try to define 'training' and we do not use rules of thumb for setting budgets or allocating training time.

One of the tenets of training at the excellent banks is the involvement of line managers in the training process. This not only keeps the training process close to the real world but is also designed to provide a useful career experience for line bankers. HongkongBank, UBS and Citibank are among those who use two to three year assignments to the training schools as a natural stage in the career development process. Others make liberal use of bankers as instructors for specific programmes. At HongkongBank and Swiss Bank Corporation, for example, half of the instructors are career bankers. It is all part of the family process at the Swiss and German excellent banks.

One of the major training challenges is keeping up with new banking products, in particular those which use technology or are securities based. Morgan's Brackenridge describes the problem:

> **The challenge is to ensure that we're up to date. Our training is very product-oriented; the typical banking officer spends at least one week a year on product training. Our courses are multi-dimensional and designed to establish links through networking. We do a lot of personal computer-based training: eventually everyone will have a PC at his or her desk.**

One of the urgent needs of the excellent banks is to bring the training function closer to the needs of the line users. Not only training in new products but also cross-training is a widespread concern. One response has been to decentralise what has been traditionally a central function. Citibank has done this for years in keeping with its decentralised culture, while Morgan, hitherto a very centralised bank, is contemplating moving more of the training function to individual business units.

Another concern is the quality of management development training. This need is particularly acute among excellent banks who have recruited primarily at the high school level. Throughout the ranks of these banks one hears of the outstanding banker who has been promoted to a management position but does not have the tools of the managerial trade: how to evaluate, coach and motivate subordinates; providing leadership; team building; setting priorities and objectives; monitoring performance, etc. Such courses are thus at the top of Citibank's training pyramid as well as a high priority at Morgan, Toronto Dominion, S-E-Banken and Swiss Bank Corporation. Texas Commerce has recently introduced its first management development programme designed for the CEOs of its subsidiary banks.

As a senior Swiss Bank Corporation planner describes the problem,

> **We have a very traditional career path: from apprentice to credit officer to credit manager to general manager. We do not move people around as in the US banks. At the top we therefore have specialists responsible for general management functions.**

Echoes Toronto Dominion's Urban Joseph:

> **We have too many specialists.**

8.3 CAREER PLANNING AND PERFORMANCE REVIEW

These concerns for cross-selling and cross-training in the excellent banks have focused attention on career path planning and management development. An enormous amount of time is spent by senior management on succession planning and development needs. Morgan, Deutsche Bank, Toronto Dominion, Citibank and others have a continuous review mechanism for management personnel which evaluates their performance, determines training needs, plots career paths and examines succession prospects. The foundation for this review is generally an annual performance appraisal based on a dialogue between supervisor and subordinate. Sigurd Schmidt describes Deutsche Bank's development planning process:

> **Every year the branches send up through the regional head branches a summary of people with managerial potential; each manager's brief is to identify his competent people. We have a standardised appraisal form, not purely MBO: we have to be careful of just producing numbers. We then rank these people – perhaps two or four from each major branch. It's an organic development, starting from the bottom and working upwards, not an automatic procedure with input from head office personnel staff only. Our universal problem is the too-benevolent manager: we in personnel have to concentrate on the objectivity of the evaluation process.**

Morgan has its own annual succession planning process conducted around the 'black book' by the Corporate Office. Sumitomo's Management Board has traditionally envisaged succession planning as its central objective. While supervisors and the personnel department evaluate a manager up to perhaps the age of forty, beyond that point he is under the eye of the Management Board. Citibank's human resource planning cycle is summarised by Rick Roesch:

We regularly review our requirements and people skills. On a semi-annual cycle, it builds up through the business units with constant adjustment and a heavy preoccupation with needs. The first review translates into our needs for people; the second, which is built around the performance review, is based on individual developmental needs.

One of the career planning techniques favoured by most excellent banks is to move potential top managers through staff jobs as well as line assignments. In large and complex organisations where the role of technology is growing, the cross-fertilisation and improved communications which result usually more than offset the inconvenience of a generalist learning a specialist assignment. At banks like Morgan, Toronto Dominion, Bank of Tokyo and Citibank, one therefore finds successful line bankers running personnel, EDP and training functions. In other banks, such an assignment would be a lateral move at best. In the excellent banks, it is recognition of the need to broaden managerial competence, improve communications and elevate the importance of key staff functions. At Toronto Dominion, Bud McMorran, head of operations and a former line banker, explains:

Operations is not a staff job in this bank – delivery is not a staff matter. In developing a system, we are bankers using technology. There's a blur in this bank between line and staff. I convey the bank to my people; I can anticipate a line banker's reaction. Both inside and outside the bank, the problem is to move the organisation to focus on the customer. We've accordingly reorganised our development activities along customer lines – wholesale and retail – so we can bring staff closer to the ultimate customer.

Other examples of cross-fertilisation abound. At S-E-Banken, EDP/Marketing head Glueck had no technical experience before taking the job. Morgan's administration head Brackenridge is a former senior lending officer. All of the Bank of Tokyo and Citibank staff officers interviewed have extensive line experience.

At the operating level, the virtues of cross-fertilisation at Morgan are described by SVP Bob McKeracher:

Planning was not our strong suit at Morgan, but it has become more serious. We use line officers on short term special assignments lasting about two years. They help design and control the planning process. We burn them out but they go back to other areas of the bank with an appreciation of how important planning is and what is required to make the process work.

Among the excellent European banks, however, cross-training for senior management is the exception rather than the rule. At Swiss Bank Corporation, for example, tradition requires that members of the Executive Board be line bankers who have come up from the apprenticeship ranks or a university background. Experience abroad in overseas branches, however, provides a significant additional career dimension. As a Vice-President of Bayerische Vereinsbank reports on his return to Munich from a New York assignment:

You finally harvest the investment in a guy going abroad when he returns home. There are so many unexploited opportunities here in the home market.

There are obviously very real constraints on cross-training. Switching relationship officers, as mentioned above, is understandably minimised. In Europe, mobility is often a problem with high potential candidates reluctant to leave the domestic charms of Munich or Geneva for even a posting elsewhere in the same country. Yet one senses that the need for broader experience, particularly at the senior management level, will move banks in this direction. Not all managers can or should be jacks of all trades, but more cross-posting would do wonders for communications and management development.

In evaluating their professional staff, the excellent banks have different views on the merits of qualitative versus quantitative performance evaluation. The split is basically between the North American banks, who generally feel that a quantitative 'management by objectives' framework is the only practical means of ranking individuals, while the Japanese and European banks are usually reluctant to commit themselves to any set of numbers. A Deutsche Bank officer would therefore be profiled solely on a variety of qualitative bases – an outgoing personality, co-operation, initiative, commitment, etc.

In Search of Excellence associates excellence with a willingness to forgive mistakes, thereby encouraging an entrepreneurial and open-minded environment. Perhaps surprisingly, there is a widely acknowledged willingness to do so among the excellent banks. The distinction made is between errors of judgement, which can be forgiven, and operating outside the process or system, which is not.

The process can be a procedural role or an unwritten understanding, but it is sacred in the excellent banks. Errors of judgement – credit, interest rate, people and product – are accepted as such, and the continued presence on the payroll of a number of interviewees for this book is evidence of this flexibility.

One of the strongest rules of the excellent game is what is called 'no surprises' at Morgan: the commitment to inform superiors as soon as a potential problem is identified. UBS' Dr Senn is quite categorical in this respect:

> **Managers can make mistakes, but they need to have the courage to report immediately so that it can be repaired at the beginning. This is better than any control system. For it, you need the courage to report your mistakes.**

Wachovia's David Cotterill emphasises the importance of trust in reconciling delegation of authority with control in the broadest context:

> **We say to our colleagues: we're interested in your problems as soon as they develop. There's no reflection on your competence; we just want to be aware of them. Through our experience we may be able to contribute to a solution. We are *not* pleased if you *don't* bring them to our attention.**

8.4 THE REWARD SYSTEM

Excellent bank compensation structures present another rich mosaic of diversity. Competitive pressures in the relevant job market, cultural values, and product focus all influence the reward system. At one extreme are the US money centre banks whose strategy is leading them to compete directly with the US investment banks for whom pay for bottom line performance is an article of faith. With varying degrees of reluctance, Morgan, Citibank and Bankers Trust have introduced bonus schemes which in some respects are comparable with those on 'the Street'. Bankers Trust's President Charles Sanford summarises this view:

> **We will provide superior compensation for superior performance and place much greater emphasis upon variable compensation tied to risk-adjusted profit contribution.**

One of the immediate lessons learned by these banks is that individual pay-for-performance bonus schemes run directly counter to a shared value culture unless they are seen to be made available to all those qualified to do the job. To avoid a divisive 'we and they' split, there has been a trend to attach bonus arrangements to specific jobs and to widen the range of eligible jobs to cover staff and commercial lending positions as well as those in a position to earn transaction or trading income. Bruce Brackenridge describes Morgan's solution:

> **We're improving our appraisal system: on a scale of 1–10, its gone from a 5 to a 7. We're close to establishing objective criteria. Incentive compensation will be available both to commercial bankers or transaction people. If the former brings in a transaction, he'll be compensated for it. We'll move people back and forth from the transaction to the relationship side, and the compensation package will vary with the job.**

Bob Russell describes Bankers Trust's approach:

> **Our MBO is tied to compensation with an emphasis on incentive as opposed to merit pay. You have to earn the former every year. We make the variable amount as much as possible of the package. The key variables are the bank's performance, the divisional performance and the individual's performance. For a very big hitter, the variable portion can be 100 per cent or more of the fixed amount, with a lot of top people in the 35–50 per cent category.**

For most of the excellent banks, such a focus on individual incentive compensation is out of the question for cultural as well as other reasons. CEOs such as John Medlin and Richard Thomson believe it flies in the face of an open, value-based culture. Wachovia's Cotterill expresses a common view:

> Wachovia does not have a bonus plan based on the volume of business produced or handled by individual employees. This is dangerous in a financial institution where qualitative factors are so critical and difficult to measure. To better assure teamwork and a proper mix of quality and quantity, competitive and merit based salaries are supplemented by incentives dependent on organisational performance. There are stock options for senior management and a savings incentive plan in which everyone shares. These, coupled with attractive employee benefits, exceptional retirement income, dependable job security and a meaningful work environment help attract and keep people of longer horizons and deeper purpose. Many of them could earn more on a current basis elsewhere, but a long-term career at Wachovia offers greater financial and psychic rewards.

Toronto Dominion has resolved the dilemma with a phantom stock plan for the top 150 officers which is expressed as a fixed percentage of salary rather than individual performance. For CEO Thomson,

> The bank makes the money, not the individual. Most people essentially want to be treated fairly. We're looking for people who want to be bankers, who want a happy place to work – not those who want to get rich quickly.

Barclays, Security Pacific and S-E-Banken have dealt with the problem by using specific affiliates in high performance sectors in which management has a share of the affiliate's profits. As SecPac's Margol puts it:

> The top 100 people by rank are not the top 100 by compensation – there used to be a total correlation. Different affiliates have different packages – fringes, salaries and bonuses. We do not wrench the organisation. If you want to move to another affiliate, we say – here's the package; no more seniority or fringes. What do you want – safety or being on the leading edge?

In addition to its willingness to offer special compensation packages to the management of its specialist vehicles, S-E-Banken has constructed a bonus plan totally outside the pay system to reward exceptional performance anywhere in the bank.

For most of the excellent European and Japanese banks, a cultural concern about incentive pay is reinforced by union-negotiated wage deals and salary scales tied to seniority and physical measurements such as branch size. Bonus programmes often exist but are either relatively small (say up to 25 per cent of salary) or are tied to exogenous factors such as dividend payout. Dr Klaus Gaertner, a SVP in Deutsche Bank's capital markets sector, describes the problem:

> **Our bonuses are tied to dividends paid and are paid roughly in proportion to salary to both staff and line officers. Individual performance is rewarded by promotion. If I bring in one Porsche underwriting, I get nothing; if I bring in several deals, I get promoted to a higher salary level at some time. A performance bonus would be a real problem – it would change the whole system for a universal bank where salary is tied to position.**

What is particular interesting about this point of view is that Deutsche Bank's universal status is the one targeted by the US commercial banks who have found it necessary to introduce incentive pay to attract and retain the necessary skills. The culture which frowns on individual performance bonuses is at least as strong in these European institutions who are major players in the capital markets.

Deutsche Bank, UBS and other European banks are prepared, however, to pay incentive compensation to overseas-based personnel, whether home country nationals or not. There is a trade-off between security and compensation. As Deutsche Bank's Gaertner points out,

> **The return ticket to Frankfurt costs something.**

For banks whose stock has performed well, stock options can be a powerful reward as well as providing ownership in the sense of common purpose. Including shares awarded, the top thirty executives own, on average, $1 million of Texas Commerce stock, while 80 per cent of the employees are stockholders.

8.5 HUMAN RESOURCE ISSUES

From this admittedly impressionistic summary of human resource practices arise three fundamental issues which are exercising the excellent banks.

The first is the gradual break-up of the family culture which has been such a strength for so long a time. The guilty party is the need to improve performance. One by one, the excellent banks are reaching the limits of profit growth through physical expansion. The US money centre banks passed this point long ago, and now it is the turn of the Japanese and European banks who have hitherto been sheltered by their strong local competitive positions.

The lifetime employment concept is threatened at the excellent Japanese banks. Sumitomo has gone over to a grading system which forces each department to rank staff on a structured A–E scale. Guidelines are established for the proportion of individuals in each grade. Even the Bank of Tokyo's Yamaguchi acknowledges that the ratio of lifetime employees at the bank will drop from 90 per cent to perhaps 70 per cent of the total. The problem will be made more acute by the decision to increase the retirement age from 55 to 60. Swiss Bank Corporation's Personnel Head Kurt Steuber sees the bank becoming

> a more aggressive employer. We're now prepared to acknowledge mistakes in promotion; people cannot assume they will keep position and rank for ever. It's a real threshold decision, a moral question for us. People after a prolonged tenure in office may no longer be as competent and flexible as they used to be. In recognition of this, we've just decided on a system of early retirement. Also we need more broadly based managers – people with potential – maybe not even with banking training.

And at Bayerische Vereinsbank, a senior personnel officer notes the

> growing pressure to be tough on people. We're not a family any more. We have to solve the problems of today and tomorrow, and we cannot solve them by postulating the family tradition.

We have to strengthen efficiency by more intensive training and letting people go.

A related issue is pay for performance. While many banks acknowledge the desirability of a bank-wide performance bonus paid proportionately to salary, bonuses for individual performance are strongly resisted in some excellent institutions in North America as well as Europe and Japan. The driving force is competition – primarily from US investment banks, but increasingly from commercial banks determined to be competitive with Wall Street.

Yet the globalisation of the securities and money markets focused on London, Tokyo and New York will place increasing pressure on all players in these markets to meet competitive compensation packages to retain their best performers. Outside hires are rare at banks like Deutsche Bank, but those hires tend to be in state-of-the-art, profit-sensitive skills. Conversely, the lure of Wall Street-type packages is having its impact even among loyal Japanese bankers as foreign securities houses enter the liberalised Tokyo market. And meeting the competition in these profit-sensitive posts will have its impact on other positions throughout the bank, as the experience of the US banks confirms.

Top managements in many non-US banks chafe under the rigid constraints imposed by a seniority and union-determined salary structure. An S-E-Banken staff officer tells of having to distribute a union-negotiated 1.25 per cent variable portion of the salary base among his middle management personnel. Dr Senn of UBS talks of possibly converting the present bonus arrangement to some kind of profit sharing for management personnel. A Swiss Bank Corporation personnel officer discusses the question of setting up special bonus plans for foreign exchange and bond dealers.

The external and internal pressures to relate more of the compensation package to individual performance are therefore growing. How far from the presently highly structured framework the European and Japanese banks will go is another issue. But a good guess is that they will find themselves drawing the same kind of distinctions prevalent in some of the more aggressive banks mentioned above.

A final issue is the availability of the necessary talent at the recruitment level. As discussed in Chapter 2, most of the excellent banks, including those like Morgan, Citibank and Deutsche Bank, whose people resources are most highly regarded, express great concern on this point. Behind their concern lie the assumption of further physical growth, with its appetite for new managerial skills, as well as a greater focus on transactional rather than traditional banking skills. In the latter respect, banks are competing with investment banks and other performance-oriented employers for a limited number of individuals, usually at the top end of the graduating class of the better business schools. Absorbing these skills in the body fabric of a 'team player' organisation will not be a totally smooth process.

9 Risk Control

The single most important credit issue is the body language of the guy in the top-corner office – it starts at the top – Larry Glenn, Citicorp.

Banks are in the business of managing risk. Traditionally this has taken the form of counterpart or credit risk, and the virility symbol of a bank has been its track record on loan quality. More recently, interest sensitivity, foreign exchange and liquidity risk have assumed greater prominence as banks – consciously or unconsciously – take major positions in these risk areas to improve profitability. Most recently, the adequacy of funding has become a very live issue for wholesale banks.

9.1 CREDIT RISK

Of central importance to the outside observer, however, is credit risk. This is what has sunk so many potentially excellent banks, and performance is relatively easily measured. From the standpoint of this book, it is vital if only because most excellent bankers acknowledge lending as their primary source of both income and risk.

If this is the case, the record of even the excellent banks as a whole seems to justify much of the external criticism of recent years. Credit losses are an inevitable by-product of the lending process, but the extent and concentration of non-performing loans since the early 1970s has caused many observers to wonder whether the term excellence can be applied to the banking sector.

Most of the excellent banks have emerged from the past fifteen years with a bit of egg on some otherwise admirable faces. The Bank of Tokyo and the New York money centre banks led by Citibank have a share of loans to troubled Latin American countries which cannot be justified by loyalty to domestic customers. Toronto Dominion, Texas Commerce, Bankers Trust, HongkongBank, S-E-Banken and the Swiss banks have all suffered from major exposures to troubled domestic clients. Sumitomo was badly embarrassed in the mid-1970s by the failure of the Ataka trading company, while Barclays suffered in the early 1980s from over-aggressive lending in the US.

Yet these excellent banks have undoubtedly learned from their experiences. Moreover, there are those like Wachovia and Deutsche Bank which appear to have sailed peacefully through these difficulties. The goal of this chapter therefore is to evaluate the risk control techniques of the excellent banks with a particular focus on the lessons learned from a very difficult period in lending history. How do the excellent banks evaluate, approve and monitor credit risk? Has any particular approach worked better than any other? What guidelines for the future have emerged from the mistakes made in the 1970s?

The common theme of credit risk control in the excellent banks is a check and balance system. Reliance is placed on the individual lending or relationship officer to identify and meet legitimate client requirements, but some form of independent check is imposed to limit errors of misjudgement, fraud, over-concentration and inexperience.

It is the form and nature of this check and balance system which differs among the excellent banks. While a wide range of practices exists, they fall roughly into two categories: one focused on individual loan officer responsibility backed up by a post-approval audit system, and a shared decision-making process where a number of staff or committee approvals are required before commitment.

The reliance on individual lending officer responsibility runs deep in the culture of the US banks as well as some other institutions. According to this culture, what attracts competent people to banking is the ability to exercise their professional judgement on credit risk relatively unfettered by the interference of those who are not as familiar with the client and local conditions. Citibank, Morgan, Texas Commerce, Hongkong-Bank and Sumitomo Bank essentially subscribe to this view. Texas Commerce's Ben Love confirms that:

> **We want room for personal initiative. The authority to lend is most precious to bankers.**

The quick response usually provided by this system is an integral part of the client strategy of many excellent banks. Deputy Chairman Purves of HongkongBank explains:

> Customers like our fast decisions on credit. Not many of our competitors can give such a quick commitment. Managers have personal lending limits, and there are no credit committees.

The system which supports this individual initiative and provides the check and balance element is described by Citibank's Larry Glenn:

> The focus is on the integrity of the decision-making process. We can accommodate a decentralised environment where everyone is driven to meet budget by making it professionally O.K. to say 'no' to certain risks. We'll fire people for failure to manage the risk process properly but not if their judgement was bad. We have over 400 senior credit officers in the bank; two of them can commit the bank up to our legal lending limit. On any new customer or loan above $25 million they need to talk to a member of the Credit Policy Committee. The system works because of a tight control on the people qualifications – we're totally unforgiving on qualifications – and we have a strong audit process.

Citibank's senior credit officers must have at least ten years of active banking experience including three years at the VP level and several lending assignments. As Citibank's John Ingraham notes,

> Senior credit officers must have a sense of caution when everyone else is enjoying the party.

Morgan also combines individual initiative with a central overview and strong credit process, as Rod Wagner explains:

> We've decentralised in the sense that we've delegated our legal lending limit to lots of people. The key is to have highly trained and sophisticated lending officers. We're centralised in that the Morgan culture calls for consultation if a deal is big or complicated. We move quickly, but we inform the institution. The Credit Policy Committee is constantly reviewing content and

policy: it makes the system think about what it's doing. It's a kind of audit which analyses what's going on in the markets and whether we're doing the right kind of business. The culture in the bank is 'no surprises': it's unacceptable to write off a loan you hadn't been concerned about. All the checks in the world won't prevent bad judgement on something like the price of oil.

Our Financial Analysis Department examines client credit quality and reports to the Credit Policy Committee; there's a healthy conflict with the Banking Department.

At Texas Commerce, a loan committee structure provides the counter-balance. Vice-Chairman Tom McDade of Texas Commerce refers to

> a religious use of committees. Most loans are approved by committees with an unanimous vote. The system ensures that people do their homework. The meetings are also open to trainees and others; they thus serve a training purpose. We also have a strong credit review process.

Sumitomo is relatively unique for a Japanese bank in granting full lending authority to the heads of its three banking groups. As in the case of Morgan, however, an informal communications system functions to inform management on the more complex or significant credits.

The majority of excellent banks prefers a collective or shared decision-making process. In some cases, this reflects the bank's centralised or shared culture. In others it represents a rejection of a more individualistic system which is perceived to have failed. A number of these banks question the wisdom of a system based on individual judgement. A senior Toronto Dominion lending officer maintains that

> the lack of individual credit authority is no problem: we can give a quick response because of our short lines of communication. It's dangerous to give marketing people lending authority. There's a shared responsibility.

Toronto Dominion's senior credit officer Ted McDowell describes the process:

There's a trade-off with unfettered lines of communications; a quick turnaround is our commitment to the field. Our credit decision makers have no accountability for business volume. There's no committee, so we get individual accountability. We have a shared decision; it is the bank's problem if something goes wrong.

Bankers Trust has recently become a convert to the philosophy of separating marketing from lending decision-making. Senior credit officer Joe Manganello explains the bank's reasoning:

Credit in the 1980s is more complex and difficult than in the 1960s for a variety of reasons. While we had a history of 'no credit committees', we found that fundamentals got ignored. We're exercised now by process and system: you need the process to ensure that the fundamentals are analysed. We now have two sign-offs: the credit officer and the relationship officer; each department has a senior credit officer. As the bank's senior credit officer, I have a quality control brief. People perceive that management wants the job done clearly and crisply. But no credit process will keep you away from judgement errors.

A strong credit process based on shared decision-making has always characterised the excellent Japanese and European banks. Ingrained in most of them is a fundamental conservatism which places depositor confidence as the central concern of the lending function. For such banks, lack of total and widespread comfort with a lending proposition essentially means a negative decision.

In the excellent Swiss and German banks, a multi-tiered process tied to size of exposure is combined with a senior Management Board-level committee to ensure that all concerned are comfortable with the final decision. The process is usually a slow-moving one, although an override mechanism is used when a quick decision is required. Management of these banks is pleased with the results and sees no particular reason for changing the system.

A typical European credit process is described by Rudolf Habicht, a Senior Vice-President in Deutsche Bank's central credit function:

> Quality of people is critical. Ours aren't necessarily better, but there's good communication with top management and a knowledge of individual credit officers. A typical career path for a staff credit man involves four years of training as a credit officer in a branch, then joining the cental credit department for three to five years. He's ready to go back to the branch system when the branches start asking his advice! We have to sell our advice to the line officers. There's a lot of reporting, but proposals are put on one page. Each member of the Board of Managing Directors signs off on credits for the geographic area he is responsible for. Very big loans have to be approved by all Board members. However, in very urgent cases, business comes before regulations, and we have enough flexibility to forget about the rules.

At Swiss Bank Corporation, a senior staff officer describes a similar process:

> Proposals by branches above their limits are reviewed centrally and submitted to the Credit Committee of the Executive Board, which meets daily. We try to respond within 24 hours of receipt of the proposal. What is unique is that each member of the Executive Board has some international responsibility so that they're all internationally-oriented.

In such a system, the chief executive or chairman usually provides the final sign-off on a major credit exposure. Union Bank of Switzerland's First Vice-President Paul Hohl summarises the process:

> Proposals go to Head Office for examination by the General Management's Loan Review organisation which evaluates the transaction and prepares a recommendation. We have no commitees. The competent General Manager decides on the proposal and sends it to our Chairman, Dr Robert Holzach, who takes a personal interest in the process. There's a heavy work-load, but I do not think we should decentralise beyond a certain size. The quality of the loan officer is decisive; we know their handwriting well.

The trade-off between responsiveness to the customer and the quality stemming from multiple review is a difficult one for any bank. The more thorough review by the excellent European banks has undoubtedly avoided errors made by using individual authorities. Yet the override system designed to short-circuit an admittedly lengthy pre-approval process functions best with well known names and risk. A European General Manager interrupted at dinner to approve a major exposure is unlikely to do so unless well briefed in advance or otherwise comfortable with the borrower.

Wachovia has developed a credit system which is designed to avoid the disadvantage of both the processes characterised above. It relies on a check supplied by senior staff officers but uses several techniques to ensure responsiveness. Chief credit officer Bud Baker reviews the system:

> In each geographic unit we have a loan administration function headed by a big warrior – a senior VP supported by a staff – who has to sign off on loans in that unit. He reports to the line unit and provides day-to-day physical contact and a link with Head Office. He's part of the team. We've pushed lending authority out into the market yet retained central control: the loan administration heads have a dotted line relation to me. The lending officers are our first line of offence and defence: there's no control credit or work-out department. We have a lot of rules. If credit is discussed in a customer call, for example, it must be documented in the file. The loan administrator gets a steady stream of information on the relationship.
>
> Our review system is formidable. There's always someone sniffing around the loan portfolio. We do not like surprises; there's never been a major loan classified by the examiner we have not identified. The system permits the CEO to put pressure on loan officers to produce; he knows that quality will be ensured.

A number of techniques have been developed which are useful regardless of the type of credit process used. While far from universally employed, there is sufficient support for them to merit some attention.

One is the alternation of line banking officers to and from the staff credit control function. Having sat on both sides of the desk goes a long way towards minimising the confrontation between advocates on a credit issue. Morgan, Citibank, Wachovia, UBS and Deutsche Bank are among those which make a particular effort in this respect.

Another is providing a positive framework within which the staff credit function operates. A legitimate concern of line bankers is the archetypal credit officer who says 'no' without suggesting how the credit might be improved or the client's needs met. To minimise this problem, Deutsche Bank's Habicht instructs his staff that

> **they have to sell their opinions on how the credit should be done to the line unit involved. I tell them that their salary depends on income received by the bank, not on deals turned down.**

In similar vein, Barclays' central advances department, which approves or disapproves credits above regional level, cannot turn down a proposal without the approval of senior line management. As Richard Carden points out,

> **they don't get cocooned in an ivory tower.**

Another technique used by a number of excellent banks who are committed to all-around lending/relationship officers is to oblige the responsible loan officer to supervise the workout of his problem loans. While this arguably is a misallocation of resources, Wachovia's Baker considers it essential

> **to understand what happens when you have to collect. We're not interested in people who just know how to sell.**

Echoes Deutsche Bank's Habicht:

> **He has to eat his own soup. It makes him a better cook.**

What have the excellent banks learned from their less than brilliant aggregate credit record of recent years? Some, like Wachovia, are proud of their record and have made no significant modifications to the credit process. Others admit to a level of concern but are not planning to revise the process. One of them, HongkongBank's Purves, acknowledges that

> We weren't particularly clever when we got caught up in the Hong Kong real estate scene in 1981. We've made mistakes. There would have been a decline a real estate prices anyway, but no one foresaw the additional impact of political developments.

Morgan's Wagner evaluates the bank's record in LDC lending:

> It was the aggregation of problems that took us by surprise. Our mistake was to assume that all the Latin American countries wouldn't be hurt by commodity prices and incorrect policies.

A Citibank EVP acknowledges that:

> We've done a lot of dumb things. We're driven by risk/reward, by an earnings per share goal.

Citibank's Larry Glenn adds:

> We've learned from the mistake of ignoring actuarial principles of risk concentration.

More specifically, Citibank's Larry Small describes real estate lending in the 1970s:

> We were euphoric over the growth of another specialised industry that was going to save us. It was called real estate. We took the biggest bath imaginable. We developed the most expensive credit training programme in the history of world banking.

Dr Guth of Deutsche Bank summarises the bank's performance in country lending and evaluating interest sensitivity risk:

> In country lending, in retrospect we went further than we would have gone for our own sake because of the great interest of our clients to export investment goods to these countries. But all of us erred in not foreseeing the combination of high interest rates and world recession. In evaluating interest rate sensitivity, we were lucky to have been very awake to the problems. We did not yet have sophisticated liability management at the time but we had enough 'nose' not to be completely wrong in our forecast. But

more importantly we made some hypothetical calculations of what a mismatch might cost and were correspondingly cautious.

A number of consequences have been drawn from the loss potential of loans made in the past decade.

First, a number of excellent banks have changed their strategy on the assumption of a relatively permanent change in the risk/reward ratio on lending as a product. Bankers Trust's views have already been quoted. S-E-Banken's Palmstierna emphasises the point:

> There's no room for risk in credit pricing. For example, we decided we wanted to be aggressive in the small corporate sector. We now see that all of our margin might be eaten up by losses. We're not withdrawing, but we have to be better equipped and know our customers better. Credit is more dangerous; there are more unexpected developments like the Swedish devaluation. Losses have increased dramatically. But we have not upgraded our procedures and quality accordingly. The key is follow up.

Toronto Dominion's President Korthals echoes the concern about a sea change in lending:

> We've lost confidence in making 100 per cent certain judgements. I was the resident hero because I forecast Chrysler's demise, but I became the goat when it survived.

Citibank's John Ingraham agrees:

> I view unsecured commercial and industrial loans as the riskiest part of commercial lending for the balance of the 1980s for all banks.

One of the conclusions drawn from this experience by many excellent banks is the need to improve the quality of credit analysis – whether it be bank, corporate, sectoral or country risk. Morgan has historically used its Financial Analysis Department of experienced analysts to backstop its lending programme.

Now others have followed. Barclays has set up a central credit review function for proposals coming up from the branches. Sumitomo has established since the Ataka failure a corporate research department to focus on sectoral analysis and provide a double check on the normal credit approval process. Union Bank of Switzerland has developed a computerised *ex-post* analysis of overall corporate and country exposure together with industry background information. Swiss Bank Corporation has a new corporate credit unit providing supplementary information and recommended guidelines for senior management on corporate exposure.

There has also been a campaign to identify problems at an early stage of their development. The 'no surprises' advocates, as previously discussed, include Morgan, Wachovia, UBS and S-E-Banken. Reading between the lines of this concern, one can imagine a variety of actual losses which could have been reduced if an alert, experienced and motivated relationship officer had blown the whistle earlier.

Risk concentration has been a source of significant losses for banks of all categories in recent years. From the excellent banks' comments, however, the issue here is more one of judgement than systems or quality of people. Whether it be sectors like energy and shipping or countries like Argentina and Brazil, very competent banks made a judgement call that went wrong. One has to assume that future potential risk concentrations in these banks will be more carefully scrutinised by credit policy units.

The need for a strong and credit check and balance system has been acknowledged by a number of excellent banks. Carried away by the need to meet profit targets and the optimism of lending officers, many banks simply did not have a strong counter-advocacy backed by the chief executive. As Wachovia's Baker points out:

> **There are too many people who are good advocates. In a lot of banks the advocates won.**

Ultimately the CEO has to carry the responsibility for ensuring this balance. Citibank's Larry Glenn maintains that

> **The single most important credit issue is the body language of the guy in the top-corner office. It all starts at the top.**

As previously mentioned, body language at Bankers Trust has been translated into a total restructuring of the credit process. While many excellent banks are not prepared to treat credit as just another product marketed by the relationship officer, there is a general recognition of the need to have some mechanism that has sufficient credibility to stand up to the enthusiastic and motivated lending function.

A final conclusion from the problems of the 1970s is the sanctity of the credit process itself. Three of the most highly regarded excellent banks – Morgan, Citibank, and Deutsche Bank – are eloquent in the importance placed on living with the spirit of the system. In these and other excellent banks, the goals of internal communication, self-review and audit, introspection into the process itself and the provision of timely information are all virtues which vie with credit judgement at the top of the bank's credit wish list.

9.2 INTEREST AND EXCHANGE RATE RISK

The risk of adverse movements of interest and foreign exchange rates is a relatively new phenomenon for the banking sector. For the excellent banks, the relevant issues have been availability of information, organisational structure and willingness to take a view on rates.

By the mid-1980s, the excellent banks had developed reporting systems which enable them to measure, on a consolidated and current basis, their sensitivity to adverse rate movements. As Deutsche Bank's experience at the end of the 1970s indicated, however, not all banks were then able to quantify their interest rate exposure. The past few years have thus seen a concentrated effort by banks to assemble the relevant information. Among the excellent banks, most have achieved this goal. Wachovia is particularly proud of its sophisticated interest exposure modelling techniques.

Organizational structure is a relevant issue in that coordination of domestic and international funding and interest rate sensitivity positions is central to low cost funds generation and intelligent management of overall exposure. The historical split between domestic and international treasury in most banks was overcome first in the excellent US money centre banks, but outside the US the process has been slower. The Bank of Tokyo's reliance on international funding has made this transition relatively simple, but in the Swiss and German banks co-ordination tends to take place on a pragmatic basis through an asset-liability management committee representing the various dealing functions.

Only a few excellent banks have no global treasury function in one form or another. One of them, HongkongBank, justifies its policy on the basis of its decentralised organisational structure. Other decentralised banks like Swiss Bank Corporation are able to gather the relevant data for decision-making but do not take their risk positions centrally.

The remaining issue in interest and exchange rate management is the straightforward one of risk/reward in forecasting future rates. The excellent banks once again reflect a wide range of risk preferences. The major US money centre and European banks run mismatch, or gap, positions naturally as a profit centre activity. For these banks, if errors are made they are judgemental in nature. Others, such as HongkongBank, Texas Commerce and Toronto Dominion, are less confident of their ability to predict rate movements and therefore run essentially matched interest rate positions.

9.3 FUNDING RISK

The issues of cost and availability of funding are implicit in the nature of banking. The portion of core, customer-derived deposits is being eroded gradually for virtually all banks. It took the Continental Illinois failure in 1984, however, to highlight the risks run by wholesale banks with a relatively high dependence on money market funds.

Most excellent banks have inherited a reasonable portion of relatively stable, low cost retail deposits in their domestic market. In the 1960s, as described earlier, Deutsche Bank and S-E-Banken made a strategic move to build a retail deposit base. Citibank followed this course at the end of the 1970s in an equally bold move away from concentration on international wholesale banking. Bankers Trust, on the other hand, moved in the opposite direction, and, together with Morgan and Bank of Tokyo among the excellent banks, faces the greatest funding challenge because of its almost total reliance upon the money markets for funding.

The challenge is being met essentially by diversification of fund sources. Overseas money and capital markets, institutional investors, and swaps are among the sources being tapped by these wholesale banks. While all the excellent banks will face growing balance sheet constraints, these wholesale institutions must place a particular priority on funding in the future.

10 Summary: The Characteristics of Excellence

The previous chapters have painted a series of portraits based on the current management practice of sixteen successful banking institutions. Superimposed upon each other, however, they present a blurred and often conflicting image. Is it possible to filter out those features which are not essential from those central to excellence? Would this produce a more meaningful and distinct characterisation?

These questions can only be answered by making some arbitrary judgements which the author has strained to avoid until now. What is central to banking excellence requires a judgement call which is made more difficult by the understandable lack of agreement on a wide sample of excellence banks. As pointed out in the first chapter, agreement among the selection panel shades off very quickly after the choice of the top three institutions. And the author is obliged to agree with some of the panelists that precious few of the excellent banks perform well on *all* of any reasonable list of criteria. What emerges is a mosaic which is pieced together empirically and is within the reach of a reasonable number of institutions. But not all sixteen of the banks score consistently well on all points.

In sum, having come this far towards the goal-line, one must make a final effort to piece together this mosaic. It will inevitably be a summary of *current* successful bank management practice. In the following chapter we shall explore how the mosaic of the future might appear.

To start with, it might be useful to summarise some of the characteristics which do *not* seem to be central to excellence. One of these is organisational structure. Banks have found a variety of ways to resolve the trade-off between geography and client, centralisation and decentralisation of credit and other decisions, and collective versus individual decision-making. These solutions reflect a variety of cultural, strategic and environmental factors, but the point is that they seem to work for the time being for the bank in question. The considerations which shape them are of far more importance from our point of view.

A second subsidiary element is the sum of the external environmental factors: regulatory constraints, nature of home market, extent of local competition, etc. Certainly it helps to be based in booming Texas or Bavaria rather than in depressed Michigan or Wallonia, but excellent managerial practices have tended to prevail over the environment. Conversely, there are many banks in these booming markets which are not considered excellent institutions. Whether one has a universal or a more limited product line, whether one is a Deutsche Bank or a Morgan, roughly the same managerial challenges must be faced. And one has only to look at the history of banks like HongkongBank, Sumitomo, Security Pacific and Bankers Trust to find institutions which have recovered strongly from a position of structural weakness or average performance within the memory of today's managerial generation.

Finally, the related variables of managerial style and level of internal stress do not seem to correlate well with excellence. At first blush, it is anomalous to bring together banks with high levels of internal tension as well as those with a relatively laid back atmosphere, with strong top-down as well as democratic leadership. Yet once again there are more important factors in the excellent banks' culture, and there is no apparent correlation of excellence with management style.

What, then, are the fundamental characteristics of today's excellent banks?

10.1 AN OPEN CULTURE

The starting point for excellence is an environment where extensive vertical and horizontal communications take place as a matter of course. Almost without exception, this quality exists in the banks analysed in this book. It would seem that an open culture is essential to sound and effective decision-making, to the communication system which unites a large and complex organisation, and to the healthy resolution of the inevitable conflicts which arise in the allocation of scarce resources.

It may well – and usually does – take more time to decide things in an open culture. Yet this is perhaps one of the more interesting findings of this research. The image of a dynamic, fast moving, entrepreneurial decision-making apparatus may be valid for a few institutions like Citibank and Hongkong-Bank, but it is clearly possible to move more slowly yet be totally competitive and successful. There are a lot of successful tortoises and unsuccessful hares in the banking business.

A variety of techniques can be used to achieve this goal. One starts with the body language of Larry Glenn's CEO: his visibility, his willingness to debate and consult, and his encouragement of others to debate and consult. Committees and *ad hoc* teams can be used as a discussion forum. Cross-fertilisation can be encouraged by moving people around as a career path device as well as bringing them together physically. But to look at the excellent banks' performance, all of this seems to happen fairly naturally if encouraged by top management.

10.2 STRONG SHARED VALUES

Within the context of this open culture, the unifying element is a strong sense of shared values throughout the managerial ranks of the organisation. Having a proud heritage is usually actively promoted by the leadership to provide positive guidance in the contemporary world. The principal means of developing such values is the excellent banks' almost universal practice of growing their own talent. This has obvious potential drawbacks, both in promoting parochial thinking today and adapting to new competitive conditions tomorrow. The latter challenges will be discussed in Chapter 11.

Yet it is difficult to see how a totally different recruitment strategy will produce the same positive results. In very basic terms, the excellent banks function effectively because their management people have gone through an intensive common learning experience and thereby developed a high level of trust and confidence in themselves and each other. How else can the conflicting demands of line and staff, of competitive claimants for resources, and of decision makers located around the globe be reconciled in a lasting and satisfying way? The obvious potential disadvantages of an inbred culture must be dealt with as a separate issue.

Not all shared values are positive in the context of today's banking challenges. Those common to the excellent banks – an open culture, a positive heritage, emphasis on quality people and performance – have survived in a Darwinian combat.

10.3 PROFIT PERFORMANCE AS A VALUE

The distinction between numbers-driven and value-driven is not a fundamental one for most excellent banks. For them, explicitly or implicitly, it is the bottom line that constitutes the relevant value. Citibank and Wachovia have articulated and actually practised non-financial values as well, while others (Morgan's focus on quality; Bank of Tokyo on pioneer spirit) have implicitly espoused them. Yet what drives the great majority of excellent banks is a satisfactory earnings trend. Such motivation is arguably weaker than that provided by non-financial values such as service and quality, but the response of most excellent banks on this question is loud and clear.

Put in perspective, a singular focus on profits represents a considerable change for many banking institutions. Physical size and market share have traditionally ranked high as bankerly priorities. A switch from asset building to profit maximisation is relatively new for the banking sector. While many excellent banks still keep an eye on their market position, the constraints on asset growth have by and large been accepted.

Excellent banks can debate among themselves the merits of various measures of profitability or the relative focus on long term versus short term profit maximisation. But accepting some form of profit maximisation as the dominant goal is a prism which focuses attention on traditional managerial policies and produces consequences which will be discussed in the next chapter.

10.4 A CUSTOMER-DRIVEN ORIENTATION

In common with the excellent companies described in *In Search of Excellence*, the excellent banks have generally oriented themselves around their customers. Perhaps a bit later than non-banks, they have segmented their markets, restructured their organisations and delivery systems to deal with the needs of particular segments, gone out to the customer to determine his needs and developed products and people skills accordingly.

Not a very revolutionary development, one might say, but a significant one for an industry historically known – with some reason – for a less than outgoing attitude to its clients. Given their relatively undifferentiated product base, the excellent banks are striving doubly hard to achieve John Rudy's goal of the answerman or problem solver. In this context, service as a substitute for product innovation is a logical development.

Many excellent banks have a long way to go to establish the level of customer interface of a Citibank or Morgan, but they are moving in the right direction. The use of account officers, better customer information and more market research are bound to become more prevalent in the future. The following chapter describes some patterns which might become more widespread.

10.5 WILLINGNESS TO INVEST IN NEW PRODUCTS

Drawing conclusions on innovation is hazardous given the uncertainties of the economic merit of new banking products and the conflict over whether being first provides a lasting competitive advantage. Yet it is quite clear that the vast majority of well-managed banks is prepared to invest considerable funds and management time when management is convinced of the merits of the project.

Citibank is perhaps unique in its total commitment to innovation, together with its philosophy of unstructured ('let a thousand products bloom') product development and its conviction that being first provides a solid competitive advantage. Most other excellent banks are either more focused, such as Wachovia, or prepared to analyse the merits of others' innovation before making a serious commitment themselves. Frequently references are made by excellent banks to instances when a competitor launched a product but was overtaken subsequently when the excellent bank introduced its own improved version. But the net result is clear. Very large, very collegial and very conservative banks have developed highly successful electronic delivery systems, innovative credit card/cheque mechanisms, interest rate swap techniques and other state-of-the-art products. It is probable that smaller, more aggressive and entrepreneurial ones could have done better, but the record of the excellent banks in product development is surprisingly good.

10.6 STRONG AND CONSISTENT LEADERSHIP

Of all the characteristics of banking excellence, it is leadership which separates the sheep from the goats. Countless banks perform well in so many respects yet do not provide a consistent game plan enforced consistently and effectively by the top management team.

The excellent banks do, and they do it without necessarily having a grand strategic scheme. What strikes the outside observer is the frequent absence of a long term planning framework – or even a detailed short term document – in the excellent banks. As George Vojta says of the quality US investment banks, strategy and planning comes from the minds of people, not from a paper document. So many of the excellent banks know implcitly who they are and where they are going. It does not necessarily have to be put on paper. It comes from guidelines established and enforced consistently by a single chief executive or collective Management Board.

Going through a major strategic exercise and putting things on paper is absolutely essential, of course, when there is a major change in direction such as has taken place in Bankers Trust, Sumitomo Bank and Bank of Tokyo. But once this has happened, the name of the game becomes execution, and any change of signals from the top corner office is usually counterproductive. This conclusion does argue for a long period in office for the top management team and for very careful attention to management succession. This task is arguably more difficult for a US bank relying on individual leadership than a collectively-managed European or Japanese bank.

The experience of the major US money centre banks seems to demonstrate the importance of such consistency. Bankers Trust is one example of a turnaround where sufficient time has elapsed to show the results of an intelligent and consistent strategy; Chemical Bank is another which could follow this path. Yet in comparison, the continuity and consistent leadership at Wachovia, whose current CEO can be regarded as the steward for over a hundred years of single-minded direction, shows what can be done.

10.7 COMMITMENT TO RECRUIT THE BEST PEOPLE

For the excellent banks committed to growing their own, the recruitment process is the keystone for investment in human resources.

Recruiting the 'best people' refers to those who are best for the particular bank's culture and strategic direction, not necessarily the 'best and the brightest'. The focus for most excellent banks will be a combination of intelligence, ability to work as a team player, adaptiveness and commitment. Some, like Citibank, will go for the over-achievers; others will be content like Wachovia to make superior bankers out of good raw material.

As will be discussed further in Chapter 11, however, excellent banks are becoming more selective in their recruiting process. The need for new skills plus the need to select out sub-par performers will have their impact on the educational as well as skills level required. To hear the chief executives of so many excellent banks place availability of the right people as their top concern for the future is sufficient rationale for including it as a criterion of excellence.

To focus on the best banks recruiting the top banking talent raises the obvious issue of entry into the charmed circle of excellence. Is it realistic to expect that such talent can be attracted to an average or even troubled bank? The answer once again lies in the track record of these excellent institutions who have themselves moved from the average or problem bank category after years of patient but persistent rebuilding. It can be done, but those who do not strive for excellence in recruiting are not likely to make it.

10.8 INVESTMENT IN TRAINING AND CAREER DEVELOPMENT

A corollary excellent trait to recruitment is a commitment to pour resources, including top management time, into the training and career development of those selected. The likely continuation of inbreeding, the role of training in improving communications, the transformation of banking products, the frequent shortfall in managerial skills and cross-training, the growing personnel selectivity – all argue for such investment.

Virtually all the excellent banks have the infrastructure and tradition for this commitment, and the establishment of training vehicles such as the Wallenberg Institute will fill the gap for those who do not. The training challenge is more one of keeping up to date on product training and developing adequate management training programmes. Given the shortage of individuals with the appropriate training and functional skills, training the trainers will be a major preoccupation.

The arguments in favour of cross-training managerial candidates are compelling. Banks like Bank of Tokyo who insist on putting university graduates in dealing and staff positions as well as line banking jobs should have a useful advantage in this respect.

It is no accident that the preoccupation of Citibank, Morgan and Deutsche Bank top management with executive succession correlates with the renowned ability of these banks to choose from a number of highly eligible candidates who will carry on the tradition of excellence.

10.9 A MATRIX-BASED MANAGEMENT INFORMATION SYSTEM

The development of product and client management information is one of the most visible current trends among the excellent banks. Some, like Citibank and Bankers Trust, have already arrived, while others are devoting considerable resources to getting there.

Developing data which will measure the attractiveness of different business segments and the performance of those responsible for them is a precondition for a client-oriented strategy as well as the effective cross-selling of products. The banks who measure performance essentially on a branch or geographic basis will find it extraordinarily difficult to motivate these units to cross-sell or execute a targeted marketing programme without the necessary functional profit information.

A corollary of this need, as Morgan's Preston has pointed out, is to separate management information from performance evaluation. Virtually all of the European banks find that almost any allocation of costs and revenues becomes a political battle. It will remain so until managers are convinced that they will be evaluated on specific performance parameters other than simply the perceived or accounting bottom line for their unit.

10.10 A STRONG AND BALANCED CREDIT PROCESS

Events of the past decade have confirmed the essential need for a respected and introspective credit process. Credit extension is still a matter of judgement, but errors in execution as well as the need for a 'what if' analysis justify a major investment in this process. Whether pre- or post-approval, the process must establish procedural rules as well as enable top management to balance the enthusiasm of lending advocates.

Some of the excellent banks have argued convincingly that the extension of bank credit has become a much riskier business and that the days of the heroic loan officer making quick commitments are numbered. Whether this is true or not, highly successful banks have managed to satisfy client needs and build profitable asset volumes without compromising a strong check and balance system.

One can also argue that the approval process of some of these slower-moving banks can be improved. Better credit training and more specialist information should assist the European banks considerably in this respect. Yet the balance of evidence, especially after the recent well-publicised credit problems of some major US banks, is that introspection and shared decisions add some very necessary value to the process.

Credit weaknesses among both excellent and other banks appear in retrospect to be a function of misuse or circumvention of a system which on paper appears impregnable. Poor documentation, unauthorised commitments, lack of follow-up, and unanticipated concentrations are some examples of misuse. The blame for such failure lies with the chief executive who sits at the middle of the 'constructive tension' described by John Medlin. Unless the CEO enforces the system, there is unlikely to be anyone else committed to the task.

The resulting profile is a somewhat different one from that of the excellent company described in *In Search of Excellence*. The objective of this volume is not to try to fit commercial banks into this mould, which is just as well because, with few exceptions, they will not fit. Only Citibank can honestly be described as effectively meeting all of the eight 'excellent' criteria set out in that book.

The excellent banks all score highly on most of the book's eight criteria. They stick to their knitting – arguably, too much so. Their shared values and open culture, together with tight credit and other controls, foster a loose–tight environment in which individuals can operate with confidence and flexibility. Their leadership, with few exceptions, is definitely of the hands-on variety with financial values driving the organisation. They believe in people, so that productivity through people is easily fostered by extensive training and the trust emanating from shared experience. And most do quite a good job of staying close to the customer.

Where things start to fall apart is the concept of lean staff and simple form. Most of the excellent banks subscribe to this doctrine, but the Japanese and European banks tend to have substantial and fairly powerful staff units in head office. And the complexity of some European and Japanese bank structures strikes at least the outsider as an impediment. But the trend is in the direction of leaner, flatter structures pushing staff functions down the line, and increased people rotation.

The excellent banks in general have real problems with a bias for action and the concept of autonomy and entrepreneurship. Apart from the overwhelming Citibank, it is hard to speak of a bias for action among the excellent institutions. To the contrary, there is probably a bias for reflection and debate in most of them. Excellent banks do communicate, use task forces and suboptimise, but the idea of firing before aiming is alien to the culture of most. As for autonomy and entrepreneurship, one can consider Security Pacific, S-E-Banken and Citibank as banks which are positively inclined towards entrepreneurial initiative and separate cultures for specific units. Failure (of the right kind) *is* tolerated, communications are intense, and product champions do exist. But the support system for these champions is strong in only a few of the excellent banks.

If *In Search of Excellence* is accused of propagating motherhood and apple pie, commercial banking might be criticised as being boring beyond words. But the excellent bankers who have read *In Search of Excellence* have found it most useful in describing good managerial practice which is as relevant to banking as to other businesses. A typical reaction is that of Bankers Trust's Al Brittain:

Everything the book said about culture were things we had stumbled upon. It was exactly the path the excellent companies had taken.

What conclusions can be drawn from these disparities between *In Search of Excellence* and the behaviour of excellent banks? Perhaps the most significant one is to focus as Bankers Trust's Brittain has on the similarities at the cultural level. There are far more similarities of excellent behaviour than differences in such cultural attributes as hands-on leadership and a focus on people. The only significant disparities lie in the areas of entrepreneurship and a bias towards action. Here there are already a few banks who espouse this philosophy, and in the future they may be joined by others. It is now perhaps appropriate to look into that future for the excellent bank.

11 Outlook: The New Global Challenges

The key is to manage *change, not* whether *to change* –
Robin Korthals, Toronto Dominion.

The preceding chapter constitutes a photograph of current management practices at the excellent banks. One of the questions posed in the interview process was how the excellent banks envisaged the future with particular reference to how these practices might evolve. The objective of this final chapter is therefore to pull together these comments and to integrate them with the author's own perception of trends in the banking sector.

First, however, some prefatory comments. The banking sector throughout the world is in a state of reasonably rapid change. The nature and rate of change is a function of local market competitive circumstances as well as willingness to change traditional behaviour. While market forces impact all banks, the rate of change may well be slower in markets where competitive pressures are perceived to be relatively weak. Nevertheless, the doctrine of challenge and response is generally a valid and universal one. Banks in most national markets are reaching the limits of profit growth through the accumulation of acceptable risk assets.

The same pressures which have obliged the New York money centre banks to re-examine their strategy will ultimately be felt in national and regional markets around the world. To the US observer, for example, the position of a leading universal German or Swiss bank in its home market may appear unassailable. Yet these banks are just as concerned about fierce competition from savings and co-operative banks as the US banks are worried about non-bank and savings bank rivals. There are very few free lunches left in the banking sectors of the developed world. One must also acknowledge that some excellent banks are well ahead of others in responding to, or even anticipating, the trends discussed in this chapter. Citibank comes instantly to mind as an industry leader, but some of its US compatriots and a few others have made significant progress in many categories.

Here are a few of the trends identified by the excellent banks.

11.1 BREAK-UP OF THE FAMILY

While in one breath the European and Japanese banks extol the virtues of a big banking family which supports all its members throughout their careers, in the next they are providing arguments for its demise.

The pressures for performance are becoming so strong in these banks that effective lifetime employment is on its way out. The cracks in the foundation of the family home are spreading, as was indicated by the quotations in Chapter 7.

One of the consequences for the European and Japanese banks who move away from lifetime employment will be the need to evaluate performance on a more quantifiable and explicit basis. At present the normal practice, as mentioned above, is a qualitative evaluation made by a superior who is often regarded as over-benevolent. While the banks may not approach the specificity of a US style MBO, there will probably be a greater emphasis on quantitative, results-oriented achievements.

Another consequence for these institutions is likely to be the demand for more information to evaluate individual performance. The present norm in these banks is profit centre data on a branch or other geographic basis. This is likely to be replaced by a matrix-type MIS based on product and client profitability so that staff as well as line officers can be appraised and priorities established.

Another bit of fallout from the family break-up could be the multiplication of specialist units with separate cultures and compensation structures. S-E-Banken and Security Pacific could thus be followed by others who are unwilling to disturb existing head office relationships but are anxious to attract and retain profit-sensitive specialists both at home and abroad.

Finally, European and Japanese banks are to a certain extent going to follow the lead of other excellent institutions by programmes of early retirement or 'windows' whereby employees over a certain age are given the opportunity to retire early on a preferred basis.

11.2 PAY FOR PERFORMANCE

A related phenomenon is likely to be a more generalised trend towards paying for performance rather for seniority, physical size of unit managed, or job responsibilities. Market forces and the need to retain people in profit-sensitive jobs have made this commonplace among the excellent US money centre banks. Banks operating in Tokyo and other major financial centres are likely to experience similar pressures.

Response to market forces may not necessarily require substantial individual performance bonuses of the type devised by the US money centre institutions. Collective bonuses for teams such as dealers or for the entire management group, along the lines of Toronto Dominion's phantom stock plan, may suffice.

In some countries, union agreements and other external constraints may slow the process. But for those banks active in the transactions sector – money and capital markets, swaps, mergers and acquisitions – being a player will require meeting the competition. And having met the competition in a specific location or product group, the experience of Morgan and others is that performance compensation must be made available to a wider range of jobs if the integrity of a single culture is to be maintained.

11.3 MORE RECRUITMENT OF OUTSIDERS

One of the excellent banks' major challenges is likely to be to increase the number of outsiders hired in mid-career without destroying the home-grown culture or losing these new people because of it. The growing importance of technology, new transactions-based products, the need for managerial skills at home and abroad – all point towards a greater openness to bringing in these new skills. Internal development might eventually provide them, but the excellent banks may legitimately prefer to move more quickly.

To a certain extent these people can be absorbed relatively easily, as has been the case in Swiss Bank Corporation, by selecting individuals who tend to fit in well with the bank's particular culture. Bankers Trust's Vojta speaks of a mentorship structure for newcomers which has worked well. But there will always be a special responsibility of the top management team to make it clear why these skills are needed and that the new recruits have their total support. Once again the body language from the guy in the top-corner office will be vital.

Over a longer period, the outside recruitment net might be spread quite wide. A Swiss head of personnel sees his bank's principal future need as the development of broad-based managerial skills:

We can only follow developments if we have people with broader academic or professional backgrounds. We need people with this potential. Maybe he won't be a banker – but we could make him a banker. Are we going about the selection process the right way?

This bridge has already been crossed by some of the excellent banks such as Citibank and S-E-Banken. Others are likely to follow.

11.4 HIGHER EDUCATIONAL STANDARDS

In similar vein, the excellent European banks and others who recruit primarily at high schools are likely to increase their hiring at university level and above to ensure a broader base of talent for managerial and specialist jobs. A combination of greater need for their skills and a tendency in many countries for talented students to acquire more formal education will drive banks in this direction.

In practical terms, this will probably require more streaming of entrants to attract the more qualified individuals as well as an attitudinal change on the part of those conducting the training. Some individuals with higher education may well be more arrogant and demanding than high school age trainees, but they must be given the challenging training format provided by the excellent US banks and others to test their capabilities.

11.5 GREATER EMPHASIS ON NON-CREDIT PRODUCTS

The pressures to diversify away from credit products are strong: the migration of quality borrowers to more attactive sources of funds, regulatory pressure to improve leverage/ gearing ratios, the competitive impact on loan margins, etc. These pressures vary according to local market conditions, and a bank enjoying satisfactory loan growth in its region is less likely to respond than, say, a money centre institution with no natural client franchise.

Yet over an extended period of time most of these banks will find that accepable growth rates can only be obtained by income diversification. Competitive pressures on the average cost of funds will reinforce this phenomenon. And 'fee-earning' products which are disguised credit products such as guaranty and underwriting commitments will not be enough.

Arbitrage products such as swaps have provided for many excellent banks a useful non-traditional supplement to the array of standard diversification opportunities: portfolio management, capital markets, corporate financial advice, stock brokerage and the like.

A new product constellation on the horizon is information. Citibank's new product strategy is heavily oriented towards the electronic delivery of information, and others will follow. Listen to one of its advocates, Thomas Glueck of S-E-Banken:

> **In the bank of the future you won't see anything except a terminal. We've neglected information economics. Bankers must understand that what they *say* to the customer is critical. We must charge for this advice. Bankers must be businesslike about it – we have something to deliver to the customer. The issue is how to price this information.**

11.6 FOCUS ON FUNDING

The excellent banks reflect widely differing degrees of reliance on non-client (essential wholesale) funding sources. Wholesale banks like Morgan, Bankers Trust and Bank of Tokyo are particularly vulnerable to shifts in preference of professional depositors. But virtually all the excellent banks are becoming more dependent on these sources of funds as asset growth exceeds that of core deposits.

There are no easy answers to this problem, but the failure of Continental Illinois has sent shock waves throughout the system. Asset accumulation has been slowed or reversed. Sources of funds in different geographic or functional markets have been tapped directly or through swaps. Liability maturities have been extended where possible.

For many banks, the pendulum has swung from asset accumulation in the 1960s and 1970s to the build-up of a reliable customer deposit base. HongkongBank's Purves agrees:

> Its an old fashioned Scottish banking principle which seems to be back in fashion. You get your deposits first, then you go and see if you can lend some money.

11.7 MORE EFFECTIVE CROSS-SELLING

The challenge of marketing products in which the salesman does not have career experience is common to the financial services industry, whether a so-called financial supermarket or a commercial bank. It demands extensive product training, strong leadership, some form of financial or non-financial motivation, and intelligent market segmentation analysis.

The excellent banks are quite clear on its importance. Dr Guth of Deutsche Bank considers it the principal challenge:

> We have to make better utilisation of the group's resources by cross-selling. There's not been enough thinking about how the various members of Deutsche Bank Group should work together. Profit centre mentality, useful as it is, can sometimes stand in the way of group thinking.

Another European chief executive, UBS's Dr Senn, agrees:

> It helps to have the product range of a universal bank, but we need more cross-selling. We need to combine different skills.

The need to integrate, to mobilise the bank's overall capabilities, is echoed at S-E-Banken. Managing Director Sven Erik Ragnar's principal concern for the future is

> to transfer the S-E-Banken spirit into the group. We need to fight the profit centre mentality. We need to cross-sell. It takes time, and it will be a bigger problem in the future.

This recognition from the top of the organisation will add to the pressures for more product training, the granting of more responsibility to account officers and the development of functional profit information to track performance. But this information must be used to manage, while performance evaluation can be tied to a totally separate data-base.

Effective cross-selling, of course, is simply another manifestation of a client-oriented or market-driven culture. Such an orientation is a matter of survival rather than excellence for commercial banks. One by one, banks are shifting from the allocation of a once-scarce resource – credit – to the marketing of increasingly differentiated products. Consumer marketing specialists with no banking experience are being recruited by the excellent banks to reinforce this client-driven culture. In the wholesale banking sector, for example, inroads made by investment banks have underlined the central importance of developing and marketing products such as swaps and currency options which meet the corporate treasurer's needs.

11.8 FOCUS ON TECHNOLOGY

The impact of communications and data processing technology is at the forefront of many excellent banks' preoccupation for the future. It requires a substantial financial commitment without assurance of technical success or incremental revenues to justify the investment. It requires developing new skills on a widespread basis. It has changed the rules of the game for delivery systems both in terms of cost-effectiveness and interface with the client.

Some excellent banks have responded positively. Personal computers are being placed at every managerial desk and PC training introduced on a corresponding scale. The segmentation of branch networks is proceeding apace. Retail customer contact through automation is being supplemented by the distribution of written communications. Most excellent banks have committed themselves to the concept of corporate client-initiated transactions through interactive terminals.

But the uncertainties abound. Loss of control to non-banks of the payments systems, with its assurance of profitable deposit float, is an issue in several countries. The outcome of integration of ATM and credit card networks is uncertain. Whose terminal will end on corporate treasurers' desks – and whether it matters – is a subject for lively discussion. The cost of developing an electronic delivery system for a smaller bank in a high cost environment weighs heavily on that bank's cost structure.

11.9 ENTREPRENEURSHIP AND BIAS FOR ACTION?

The relative absence of the two qualities of a bias for action and entrepreneurship was noted in Chapter 10. In the future, one can argue that more excellent banks will join the present handful which are distinguished by these qualities.

In wholesale banking, the challenge of the capital markets and the example set by the US investment banks will exert compelling pressures in this direction. The bias for action of these institutions, for example, has been central to the instantaneous exploitation of product and market 'windows' in the global capital markets. The trend towards a transaction rather than relationship – based strategy will reinforce such a bias.

As for entrepreneurship, the recruitment of more highly qualified bankers who are paid for performance will almost inevitably lead to a higher valuation of entreureneurial qualities. Other excellent banks will thus join Citicorp, S-E-Banken and Security Pacific in their encouragement of this initiative. Whether the subject is product development, trading initiatives or distribution ideas, the entrepreneurs in Salomon Brothers and Credit Suisse First Boston represent impressive peer models for their banking competitors.

11.10 A TESTING OF THE CULTURE

The sum total of these challenge is, for most excellent banks, a direct confrontation with its traditional culture. Top managers at Barclays, Sumitomo, Security Pacific, Morgan and HongkongBank express concern as to whether the two are compatible.

Bank of Tokyo talks of reducing its personnel by 1000 to 5000 – a rude shock for a lifetime employer. HongkongBank wrestles with defending a federalist autonomy against integrated competitors. One of its senior officers wonders out loud whether line bankers will be prepared to sell packaged products:

> **it's like moving them from Harrod's to Sainbury's.**

A friend at Texas Commerce worries openly about US banking deregulation and its impact on the Texas market. Morgan's Brackenridge sees adaptation to the 'investment banking syndrome' as the bank's greatest challenge. Sumitomo's Managing Director Hiroshi Mineoka describes his bank's recent acquisition of Banca del Gottardo, a traditional Swiss bank as:

> **a magnificent experiment. Our culture works well now. We want to become internationalised, so we made the acquisition. But we may reach a limit to this internationalisation.**

There will doubtless be several cultures which cannot stand the strain. Yet the history of these same excellent banks is replete with examples of successful adaptation. Hongkong-Bank has survived over 100 years of change, including a major change of direction in the 1950s after moving from Shanghai. Morgan's culture survived the merger in 1959 with Guaranty Trust. Citibank has gone heavily into retail, largely with outside recruits, while Bankers Trust has successfully dropped retail banking in favour of merchant banking. The combination of strong and consistent leadership, good people and an open culture can do a lot to absorb shocks.

Whatever the outcome, these are universal concerns for the excellent banks. One can assume that technological issues will occupy significantly more senior management time than in the past.

All of these ten issues are of importance to the banking community as a whole, not just the excellent institutions. How well they respond to them will determine the selection of the excellent banks of the future. But perhaps most relevant is the point made by Toronto Dominion President Korthals:

> **The key is to *manage* change, not *whether* to change.**

The head of strategic planning of one of the excellent Continental European banks sums up an outlook which is reflected in comments from a number of others:

> **Our basic need is to harness our potential. The Management Board is ready for new ideas; they're sending signals to management. We have a dynamic culture – our fault, if anything, is impatience. Our structure won't change, even though it's a very time consuming way to run a bank. We'll hire more non-bankers, but the core will always be branch managers who will be trained in different products and geographic markets.**

In concluding this book, one is conscious of the dangers of appearing to homogenise excellent banks from a wide variety of markets and traditions. Each bank has responded, and will continue to respond, to challenges in its own way. The initial wave of banking internationalisation, which involved overseas physical expansion of networks and assets, has reached its peak and is now on the ebb tide. A second global tide of managerial practice and challenges is now building. It is a tide of technology, information systems, product diversification, human resource development and funding sources. Response to these challenges will separate the excellent banks of the future from the also-rans.

Index of Bankers

Abs, H. 24

Baker, B. 24, 109, 110, 113
Beim, D. 28, 48, 58
Brackenridge, B. 18, 21, 23, 48, 58, 71, 92, 97, 136
Braddock, R. 86
Brittain, A. 29, 70, 78, 81, 127
Brupbacher, W. 46–7

Carden, R. 26, 31, 47, 110
Cotterill, D. 96, 98

Flamson, R. 72, 82

Gaertner, K. 99
Galliker, F. 19, 75
Glenn, L. 21, 71, 105, 111, 113, 119
Glueck, T. 46, 132
Gubert, W. 48
Guth, W. 17, 18, 55, 68, 69, 73, 75–6, 78, 111, 133

Habicht, R. 107, 110
Hartmann, R. 30, 51
Heilshorn, J. 25, 33, 36, 54, 57, 67, 71
Hohl, P. 108

Ingraham, J. 105, 112

Jacob, W. 89, 90
Jones, T. 49, 69
Joseph, U. 67, 93

Knief, B. 49, 52, 59, 63, 86
Korthals, R. 40, 82, 88, 112, 137

Love, B. 53, 77, 79, 82, 86, 104
Lütolf, F. 81

McDade, T. 106
McDowell, T. 22, 107
McKeracher, R. 34, 64, 94
McMorran, B. 94
Malmstroem, C. G. 59
Manganello, J. 107
Margol, I. 29, 98
Medlin, J. 16, 24, 37, 43, 59, 69, 76, 82, 88, 90, 98, 126
Mineoka, H. 136

Olsson, C. G. 26, 30–1, 37, 76, 82, 90

Palmstierna, J. 30, 46, 60, 80
Peters, T. ix, 1
Peterson, D. 42
Preston, L. 17, 43, 78, 84, 89
Purves, W. 24, 26, 85, 105, 110, 133

Ragnar, S. E. 134
Reed, J. 49
Roesch, R. 16, 18, 49, 66, 86, 91, 93
Roth, N. 39
Rudy, J. 55, 64, 121
Russell, R. 61, 97

Sandberg, M. 47, 79
Sandstroem, A. 90
Sanford, C. 97
Schmidt, S. 89
Senn, N. 25, 42, 54, 77, 85, 96, 134
Small, L. 54, 111
Smith, P. 70
Smith, R. 29
Spanier, H. 57
Steuber, K. 100

Takai, K. 44, 66, 86
Thomson, R. 19, 39, 58, 70, 79, 82, 98
von Tucher 24
Tyndall, M. 15

Umemoto, F. 66

Van Hooven, E. 21, 23, 45

Vojta, G. 28, 37, 122, 131

Wagner, R. 21, 111
Watanabe 80
Waterman, R. ix, 1
Wriston, W. 18, 24, 86

Yamaguchi, T. 36, 100

Index of Subjects

Bank of Tokyo
  account officers in   56
  centralised decision-making   66, 68
  communications   19
  heritage of   23, 24
  international funding, reliance on   115
  lifetime employment in   100
  loans to Latin America   103–4
  recruitment in   25, 86, 124
  strategic planning by   36
Bankers Trust
  chief executive's role in   78
  credit problems   104
  credit risk control   107, 114
  customer segmentation in   61
  new value system   28–9, 30, 31
  organisational change in   70
  product innovation in   48
  recruitment by   84, 131
  relationship officers in   58
  reward system in   97
  and risk of funding   115–16
  strategic planning by   37, 38
  banking sector, trends in   128–37
    cross-selling   133–4
    cultural confrontation   136
    entrepreneurship   135–6
    family break-up   129–30
    funding   133
    higher education requirements   131–2
    non-credit products   132
    recruitment of outsiders   130–1
    reward schemes   130
    technological trends   134–5
Barclays Bank
  assets   8

credit problems   104
credit control   110, 111–12
and cultural change   31
decentralisation in   26–7
managerial strength   81
product innovation   47
relationship management   56
Bayerische Vereinsbank
  career planning in   95
  centralised decision-making   66
  employment policies   100–1
  financial values of   15
  heritage of   24
  recruitment by   85–6
  relationship management   56
  strategic planning by   34, 38
bonus schemes   97

Canadian banking
  cross-training in   94
  and relationship management   57
capital markets sector
  innovation in   47–8, 51
  recruitment from   84
career planning   93–6
  and cross-training   94
  importance for excellent banking   124
centralisation   65, 66–7
check and balance system   104, 113
  lending officer's role in   104, 107
Chemical Bank   123
chief executives, role of   74–82
  common aspects of   79–82
  communications role   78
  and conflict resolution   76–7
  as credit decision maker   78
  as deal-maker   79
  in German and Swiss banks   74–6

Index of Subjects

Citicorp (Citibank NA)
  career planning 93–4, 124
  credit risk control 105, 111, 112, 113
  customer contact 54–5, 57, 59
  customer segmentation 61, 62–3
  decentralisation 25–7, 36–7, 65–6, 67
  excellence of 126–7
  heritage of 24
  and individual decision-making 67
  internal conflict in 71
  Latin American loans 103–4
  and matrix management 69
  non-financial values of 16, 120
  and organisational change 70
  product innovation 48–9, 121
  recruitment by 25, 86–7
  and risk of funding 115
  strategic change in 38
  training in 91, 92
communications 18–23, 67–8, 72–3
  chief executive's role in 78
  and conflict resolution 71
  between management and trainees 89–90
conflict resolution
  by chief executive 76–7
  through communications 71
credit analysis, improvement in 112–13
credit granting 78–9
credit officer 104, 105, 107
credit risk 103–14
  and check and balance system 104, 113
  concentration of 113
  loan officers and 104–5
  and need to improve credit analysis 112–13
  and shared decision-making 105–7
  techniques for control of 109–11
cross-selling 50–1, 93, 125
  future trends in 133–4
cross-training 94–5
culture
  change in 27–31, 136–7
  need for open culture 118–19
customer information 63–4

customer relations
  customer segmentation 60–3, 121
  proximity to customer 53–60
  through market research 59–60
  through organisational restructuring 58–9
  through relationship officer 55–8

decentralisation 25, 62
  and credit risk control 105
  and internal conflict 71
  as strategic planning concept 36–7, 65–7
decision-making
  collective 67–8, 106–7
  individual 67–8, 104–6
  and informality 18–23, 67–8, 71–2
  see also centralisation, decentralisation
delegation see decentralisation
delivery systems 45–7, 51
Deutsche Bank
  career planning in 93
  collective decision-making in 67, 71
  communications in 19, 20, 23
  cross-selling 133
  credit process 107–8, 110, 111
  customer contact 55, 59
  and account officers 56–7
  customer segmentation 60–1, 62
  decentralisation in 26, 67
  heritage of 24
  and interest rate risk 114
  leadership of 75–6
  and organisational change 69–70
  performance evaluation in 95
  product innovation in 45–6
  recruitment by 25, 84, 87, 124
  reward system in 99
  and risk of funding 115
  strategic planning 34, 35
  training in 89
domestic branch network 62

EDP 45–6
education
  future trends in 131–2
  requirements for banks 87–8

Index of Subjects

Egon Zehnder Survey ix, 4
entrepreneurship 88, 135–6
European banks
  collective decision-making in 67, 71, 73
  credit process in 107–9
  cross-training in 95
  and customer profitability information 63
  geographic-oriented structure 62
  lifetime employment and 129, 130
  performance evaluation by 95
  reward system in 99
  universal banks 51
excellent banking
  chief executive's role in 74–82
  and cultural change 27–31
  and customer relations 53–63
  definition, problems of 1–3
  description of 5–8
  features of 117–24
  financial performance 8–9, 12–13
  future trends in 128–37
  human resources' contribution to 83–102
  list of 3–4
  organisational structure of 65–73
  and product innovation 42–52
  and risk control 103–16
  shared values of 14–27
  strategic planning in 32–8

family culture 90
  break-up of 100
  future trends in 129–30
financial performance
  and excellence in banking 8–9, 12–13
  measures of 8
  by peer group 9–12
  problems of quantifying 8–9
funding
  future trends in 133
  risk of funding 115–16

geographic location 8, 68
German banks 128
  credit risk 107
  earnings of 9
  lack of leadership in 74–6, 77

organisational structure in 68
recruitment by 87
strategic planning in 35
training in 89, 91
work load 80

heritage of excellent banks 23–5
HongkongBank
  chief executive's role in 79
  and credit risk 104, 105, 110–11
  and cultural change 29, 136
  decentralisation in 26
  heritage of 24
  individual decision-making in 67
  and interest rate risk 115
  pressure of work in 27
  product innovation in 47
  recruitment by 25, 85, 88
  strategic planning by 34, 35
  training in 90, 91
  view of mission statements 39
human resources
  career planning and performance review 93–6
  employment policies, changes in 100–1
  importance of for excellent banking 17–18, 83–102
  reward systems 96–100
  salary structure changes 101
  selection of 84–8
  talent 102
  training 88–93

In Search of Excellence ix, 1, 2, 3, 15, 42, 50, 53, 64, 69, 96, 126, 127
industry/sectoral specialisation 63
innovation *see* product innovation
Institutional Investor 12
interest and exchange rate risk 114–15

Japanese banking
  centralisation in 66
  conflict resolution in 71
  and customer profitability information 63
  innovation in 44–5
  lifetime employment in 100, 129, 130

recruitment by 87
relationship management 56–7
restructuring problems of 69
reward system in 99

Latin America, loans to 103–4
leadership 24, 74–82
   common aspects of 79–82
   lack of 74–6, 77
   as requirement for excellent banking 122–3
   types of 74–9
lending officer *see* credit officer
lifetime employment 100, 129, 130
loan committees 106

management information 63
   future trends in 129
   matrix-based 124–5
market research 59–60
matrix management 69, 124–5
mission statements 38–9
Morgan Guaranty Trust
   career planning in 93, 94–5, 96
   centralised decision-making 66
   communications in 21, 23, 78
   credit risk control 105, 111
   cross-selling 50–1
   customer contact 54
   customer profitability information 64
   formation of Banking Division 61–2
   heritage of 24
   mission statements, view of 39
   and organisational change 70, 71
   and product innovation 43–4, 48
   professional skills, importance of 17, 18
   recruitment by 84, 88, 124
   relationship officers in 57–8
   reward system in 97, 130
   strategic planning 34–5
   training in 89, 92

non-credit products 132

organisational structure 65–73
   attitudes to changes in 69–71
   communications and internal conflict 71
   decentralisation 65–7
   as feature of excellent banks 117–18
   geographic location and client 68
   individual and collective decision-making 67–8
   and interest rate risk 114
   and matrix management 69

peer group analysis 8–9
performance evaluation 95–6, 125
   future trends in 129
product diversification 8, 42
   by acquisition 50
   future trends in 132
product innovation 42–52, 121
   in capital markets-related sector 47–8, 51
   disadvantages of 42–3
   in Japanese banks 44–5
   selective innovation 43–4
   in technology-based delivery systems 45–7, 51
profit increases 120
   as motive in excellent banking 15, 36

recruitment strategy 25, 84–8, 119
   educational requirements 87–8
   and entrepreneurial skills 88
   for excellent banks 123–4
   future trends in 130–1
   qualities required 85–7
   and value sharing 84–5
relationship officers 55–7
   weaknesses of 57
ROA (return on assets) 3, 8
ROI (return on investment) 3, 8
   as objective of excellent banks 15
reward system 96–100
   future trends in 130
risk control 103–16
   credit risk 103–14
   funding risk 115–16
   interest and exchange rate risk 114–15

Index of Subjects

salary structures 101
S-E-Banken
  chief executive's role in 76
  credit pricing in 112
  credit problems 104
  cross-selling 134
  customer segmentation 61
  customer survey of 60
  decentralisation in 26
  and different cultures 30–1
  product innovation in 46
  reward system in 99
  and risk of funding 115
  strategic planning by 35, 37
  training in 90
Security Pacific (SecPac)
  communications in 72
  new value system 28, 29–30
  product expansion in 50–1
  product innovation in 42–3
  recruitment by 84, 88
  reward system in 98
size, management of 5–8
staff functions 66, 67
strategic planning 32–40
  and decentralisation 36–7
  direction of 35
  disillusionment with long range planning 37
  executive involvement in 38
  and financial projections 34
  in form of scenarios 34–5
  medium-term planning 35–6
  and need for change 36, 38
Sumitomo Bank
  career planning in 93
  communications in 20
  and credit risk control 106, 113
  corporate banking division 61
  heritage of 23, 24
  relationship officers in 56
  staff ranking 100
  strategic planning in 35
Swiss banks 128
  credit risk and 104, 107
  earnings of 9
  lack of leadership in 74–5
  organisational structure 68
  recruitment by 87–8

training in 89, 91
work load in 80
Swiss Bank Corporation
  career planning in 95
  chairman's role in 74–5
  collective decision-making in 67
  communications in 20–1, 22–3
  credit process in 108, 113
  decentralisation in 26, 62, 67
  employment policies 100
  and interest rate risk 115
  product innovation 46–7
  recruitment by 25, 87, 88, 131
  strategic planning by 35
  training in 91

technology, future impact of 134–5
Texas Commerce
  communications in 22
  and credit risk control 104, 106
  customer contact in 53–4
  financial values of 15
  heritage of 23
  and innovation 42
  leadership in 71–2, 76
  recruitment by 86, 88
  strategic planning by 34, 38
Toronto Dominion
  career planning in 94
  centralisation in 67
  chief executive's role in 79
  communications in 19–20, 22
  credit problems of 104
  credit risk control 106–7, 112
  mission statements, view of 39–40
  and organisational change 70
  product innovation 47
  recruitment by 88
  relationship management 58–9
  reward system in 98
  strategic planning by 37
training 88–93
  as communications vehicle 90
  line managers' involvement in 91
  management development training 92
  need for excellent banking 124
  top management involvement in 89–90

Index of Subjects

Union Bank of Switzerland
  centralised decision-making in   66
  chief executive's role in   77
  credit process in   108, 113
  cross-selling   134
  customer contact   54
    and market research   59–60
  innovation, views on   42
  recruitment by   25, 85
  reward system in   99
  training in   89, 90
US banking
  cross-training in   94–5
  importance of   5
  and interest and exchange rate risk   114–15
  and organisational change   69
  performance evaluation in   95
  and relationship management   57
  segmentation in   63

values
  financial values   15–16, 120
  leadership and   79
  new value systems   27–30
  non-financial values   16
  decentralisation   27
  heritage   23–5
  pressure to perform   27
  professional skills   17–18
  recruitment policies   25
  total communication   18–23
  shared values   14–15, 119–20
  and recruitment   84–5

Wachovia
  credit process in   109, 110, 113
  heritage of   23
  and innovation   42, 122
  and interest rate risk   114
  leadership in   123
  and mission statements   38
  non-financial values of   16–17, 120
  organisational change   69
  and Personal Banker   57, 59
  recruitment by   88, 123
  relationship management   57, 58
  reward system in   98
  strategic planning in   37